Why do I keep doing tnis?

Social Responsibility Therapy: Understanding Harmful Behavior Workbook 2

James M. Yokley, Ph.D.

This workbook focuses on developing an understanding of "The Stress-Relapse Cycle " that maintained unhealthy, harmful behavior. Case study examples for the intervention summaries in Exhibits 1- 3 in this workbook are described in Chapter 2 of the Social Responsibility Therapy treatment manual and in The Clinician's Guide listed in the references section.

The Social Responsibility Therapy focus on Understanding Harmful Behavior through "The Problem Development Triad" includes a three workbook series designed to help individuals with unhealthy, harmful behavior understand how they got that problem, what kept it going and how it spread to other areas.

Workbook 1- "How did I get this problem?" focuses on understanding how unhealthy, harmful behavior was acquired through The Risk Factor Chain

Workbook 2- "Why do I keep doing this?" focuses on understanding how unhealthy, harmful behavior problems were maintained by The Stress-Relapse Cycle

Workbook 3- "How did my problem spread?" focuses on understanding how unhealthy, harmful behavior problems were generalized to other areas using The Harmful Behavior Anatomy

---

A Social Solutions Healthy Behavior Lifestyle Development Project

---

Social Responsibility Therapy Mission Statement:
"Reclaiming Dignity through Honesty, Trust, Loyalty, Concern and Responsibility"

Information on Social Responsibility Therapy is available at www.srtonline.org. The Social Responsibility Therapy treatment manual for adolescents and young adults, Social Responsibility Therapy workbooks and The Clinician's Guide are available at www.socialsolutionspress.com

Published by
Social Solutions Press
Post Office Box 444
North Myrtle Beach, South Carolina 29597
Third Printing

Who can benefit from this workbook?

Individuals with unhealthy, harmful behavior- Those who are uncertain of what maintains their harmful behavior can benefit from the "Structured Discovery" approach of this workbook with assistance from their therapist. In addition, those who are aware of some contributing factors but do not have a full understanding of "Why do I keep doing this?" are also likely to benefit. See summary on back cover.

Mental Health Professional use in treatment plans and programs- The Awareness Training Goal for those who complete this workbook is to understand how they maintained their problem behavior. The objectives are to complete each of the five phases in "The Stress-Relapse Cycle " and give at least one specific example of a healthy behavior success skill that can be used to break the cycle at each phase. Since the focus of this workbook is on the primary contributing factors that maintain multiple forms of unhealthy, harmful behavior, it is ideal for those who have a co-occurring harmful behavior in addition to the one that resulted in their referral for treatment. The increased workbook structure includes step-by-step self-discovery directions. This "Structured Discovery" approach addresses the self-awareness problems exhibited by many individuals with unhealthy, harmful behavior. This Structured Discovery workbook is helpful for those with strong autonomy needs who value their independence, like to work on their own, take charge of their lives and help themselves deal with their own situations. It is ideal in limited resource public service or institutional settings that require group treatment by clients who must contribute to their treatment plans and support each others goals.

Harmful behavior is unhealthy, excessive, compulsive or abusive and harmful to self or others. Social Responsibility Therapy (SRT) has a strong focus on developing honesty, trust, loyalty, concern and responsibility as competing responses to harmful behavior. These multicultural prosocial values are the healthy relationship success skills that employers, parents, partners and probation/parole officers are looking for in their workers, children, relationships and parolees. SRT is highly consistent with the family values of faith-based treatment organizations as well as the "Right Living" treatment approach of Therapeutic Communities and Twelve-Step Programs. The SRT healthy relationship and behavior success skills focus meets the rehabilitation goals of correctional institutions and social service group homes making it easy to integrate into those settings. This workbook is best suited for individuals over age 13 with good reading ability and basic arithmetic skills. Although developed for use with therapist input to help those in treatment become more active participants, it can also provide self-awareness and motivation for those considering therapy. The three SRT workbooks on understanding harmful behavior were originally intended to be used consecutively but can used individually for treatment focused on insight (workbook 1), relapse prevention (workbook2) and co-occurring problems (workbook 3).

Mental health professional information on how to use this workbook is outlined in Appendix A. Workbook support materials listed in the references section include: A step-by-step clinician guide for implementing each workbook section and users guide for the healthy behavior success skills described in the workbook; A workbook development manual documenting the research support for each workbook section and; Social Responsibility Therapy treatment manuals for adults, adolescents and preteens.

Social Responsibility Therapy (SRT) Acknowledgements

A special thanks to: Christine Laraway and Brigette Bulanda for their help in implementing SRT with adolescents in Forensic Foster Care; Jennifer LaCortiglia for her help in adapting SRT for preteens; Rose Chervenak for her help in providing SRT to adolescents referred for sexual behavior problems in the residential Therapeutic Community setting; Chris Hewitt for his help in presenting Social Responsibility Therapy (SRT) to residential substance abuse clients and; Angie Roth for her program coordination of SRT for obesity patients in hospital-based treatment. Their feedback on the use of this workbook with clients exhibiting multiple forms of harmful behavior provided highly valuable treatment information.

Understanding How Harmful Behavior was Maintained: Social Responsibility Therapy Awareness Training Workbook 2

Table of Contents   **Page**

Introduction to Social Responsibility Therapy & Understanding Harmful Behavior

Social Responsibility Therapy Summary 1

History of Harmful Behavior 4

Introduction to The Problem Development Triad 7

Getting what we want in life 10

Summary of Healthy Relationship and Behavior Success Skills 17

The Problem Development Triad Section 2-
How Harmful Behavior was Maintained

Understanding How Harmful Behavior was Maintained: The Stress-Relapse Cycle 29

    Phase 1- Negative Coping 35

    Phase 2- Cover Up 41

    Phase 3- Stress Build-Up 49

    Phase 4- Slip (lapse) 59

    Phase 5- Fall (relapse) 75

Life Impact Statement: The Stress-Relapse Cycle 88

Workspace 99

The Stress-Relapse Cycle Worksheet: How Harmful Behavior was Maintained 101

Footnotes and References 103

Table of Contents

Page

Tables

Table 1. The Harmful Behavior Continuum: Selected Behavior Examples 2
Table 2. Who we are According to Aristotle 10
Table 3. Summary of What We Want from Others 11
Table 4. SRT Opposite Extreme Values and Behaviors 15
Table 5. SRT Opposite Extreme Positive Rules 15
Table 6. Opposite Extreme Healthy Behavior Success Skills 16
Table 7. Healthy Behavior Success and Relationship Skills Cue Cards 27
Table 8. Three Basic Types of Negative Coping: Selected Harmful Behavior Examples . . 35
Table 9. Going to the Opposite Extreme with Positive Coping 39
Table 10. Going to the Opposite Extreme by Opening Up 46
Table 11. Going to the Opposite Extreme with Stress Adaptation 54
Table 12. Relieving stress with The ABC's of letting feelings go 55
Table 13. Going to the Opposite Extreme by Stepping Up Relapse Prevention 67
Table 14. Relieving high risk emotions: The ABC's of letting feelings go 73
Table 15. Slip Give Up Trigger Examples across Harmful Behaviors 76
Table 16. Typical Consequences of Taking a Fall into Harmful Behavior 77
Table 17. Emotional Rumination: Summary Across Harmful Behaviors 79
Table 18. Blocking the Slip Give Up Trigger and Breaking a Fall 87
Table 19. Combined Contributors to taking a Fall (relapse): Selected Examples 96
Table 20. Going to the Opposite to Recovery from Harmful Behavior 97

Exhibits

Exhibit 1- Managing Risk Factors for How Harmful Behavior was Acquired:
The Risk Factor Chain 104
Exhibit 2- Recovery Behavior Maintenance: The Stress Management Cycle 105
Exhibit 3- Addressing Factors that Support Multiple forms of Harmful Behavior 106

Figures

Figure 1. The Problem Development Triad 8
Figure 2. The Prevention or Development of Harmful Behavior 9
Figure 3. Stress-Relapse Cycle Summary 16
Figure 4. How Harmful Behavior was Maintained: The Stress-Relapse Cycle 34

Appendices

Appendix A- Information for Mental Health Professionals 107
Appendix B- Self-Awareness Problems and Relapse:
       Foresight Deficit Decisions 110
Appendix C- Types of Irresponsible Thinking and Responsible Alternatives. 114
Appendix D- Summary of Situation Response Analysis and
       Situation Response Analysis Log 127
Appendix E- Social Responsibility Therapy Self-Evaluation 131
Appendix F- Awareness and Honesty Examination 132

Social Responsibility Therapy Manual Description 141

Workbook Series and Order Information 143

Introduction to Social Responsibility Therapy and Understanding Harmful Behavior

"If you're not working on the solution, you're part of the problem" -- Eldridge Cleaver [1]

Note: Review this section and update your answers even if you have completed workbook 1.

Social Responsibility Therapy Summary

Social Responsibility Therapy addresses multiple forms of unhealthy, excessive, compulsive or abusive behavior that is harmful to self and/or others (i.e., "harmful behavior"). Traditional treatments typically focus on helping yourself. Social Responsibility Therapy focuses on helping yourself and others. In Social Responsibility Therapy, learning to care for yourself and others involves developing enough social maturity (i.e., honesty, trust, loyalty, concern and responsibility) and emotional maturity (i.e., self-awareness, self-efficacy/confidence and self-control) to avoid behavior that is unhealthy to you or harmful to others. Social Responsibility Therapy teaches multicultural prosocial values and behaviors that help prevent unhealthy, harmful behavior. In Social Responsibility Therapy, "If you're not working on the solution, you're part of the problem". If part of the problem is that unhealthy, harmful behavior got in the way of your education, work on the solution by reading this workbook with a dictionary and educate yourself by looking up the words you don't know.

What's in it for me? Less unhealthy, harmful behavior results in less consequences and a more healthy, positive life. More unhealthy, harmful behavior leads to more consequences and a less healthy, negative life. Unless you are keenly aware of your thoughts, feelings and motivations, you will make decision mistakes or slips that lead to "relapse" and falling back into unhealthy, harmful behavior. One type of decision that leads to relapse involves a problem with awareness referred to as a "foresight deficit decision" or foresight slip. Foresight is the ability to look ahead and think about what could happen in different situations. A foresight deficit decision often results in thoughtless decisions to enter high risk situations for slipping into harmful behavior. If you were ever asked, "What were you thinking?" you probably had a foresight slip into trouble. This is a very serious matter. Since your decisions control the path that your life will take, you need to locate the type of harmful behavior you want to change or that resulted in your referral for treatment in Appendix B (p. 110) and study the examples of decisions that led to relapse by individuals who lacked foresight and self-awareness. Don't worry if the connection between the decisions and the relapse that occurred is not clear to you right now. The primary purpose of this workbook is to help you develop enough self-awareness to make those connections and avoid falling back into harmful behavior or developing a new one after you have successfully stopped this one. Although you can use this workbook as a self-help tool to develop your own awareness and understanding of yourself, it is typically used in individual/family therapy or in group treatment programs and you are likely to benefit from therapeutic discussion of each section with others. The unhealthy, harmful behavior targeted by Social Responsibility Therapy covers a broad spectrum of behavior on the Harmful Behavior Continuum (Table 1) ranging in Social Responsibility impact from primarily hurting self (e.g., excessive eating or skipping medication) to hurting self and others (e.g., substance abuse or gambling debt) to primarily hurting others (e.g., acts of physical or sexual aggression) and in severity from relatively mild to socially devastating. The multiple forms of abusive behavior that Social Responsibility Therapy targets includes: trust abuse (e.g., lying, cheating, confidence scams, running away); substance abuse (e.g., drugs/alcohol, cigarettes, unhealthy eating); property abuse (e.g., theft, vandalism, fire setting, excess spending/shopping, gambling debt); physical abuse (e.g., school bullying, assault, kidnapping, robbery) and; sexual abuse (e.g., rape, child molestation, harassment).

Table 1.   The Harmful Behavior Continuum: Selected Behavior Examples

Primary Area of Impact ⟶

Behavior Impact Severity	Harmful to Self	Harmful to Self and Others	Harmful to Others
	Unhealthy Eaters (Overeat/binge/purge/starve) **Medication Non-compliance** **Self Injury/Cutting** **Nicotine Abusers**		
	Workaholics (Single) (with partners or family)		
	Codependents (Self-destructive relationships) (Abuse enablers)		
	Sexual Compulsives (Deviant masturbation, porno) (Unprotected sex, affairs, prostitution)		
	Money Abusers (Single shopaholics) (Gamblers with partners/family) (Embezzlers, Credit fraud)		
	Substance Abusers (Single alcohol and drug abusers) (Alcohol and drug abusers with partners/family) (Drunk drivers, Drug dealers)		
	Responsibility Abusers (Work Neglecters) (Child Neglecters)		
	Trust Abusers (Partner cheating) (Professional con artist)		
			Verbal/Power Abusers (employee harassment) **Property Abusers** (theft, vandalism, arson) **Physical Abusers** (bullying, assault, child abuse) **Sexual Abusers** (rape, child molestation) **Contract Killers** **Lust Murderers, Serial Killers**

Source: Adapted with permission from Table 1.1 in Yokley (2008)

Note: "The more difficult the problem, the harder it is to change" may not always be the case. Less severe harmful behaviors which impact less people can be more difficult to change because of…

1. Impact Rationalization- It's low on the social impact continuum, e.g., "It doesn't hurt others, it only hurts me"
2. Availability and associated Normalization- It's normal to eat, smoke, spend and sometimes over do it, e.g., "Everyone does it" or "Lots of people do it". For example, smoking lapses "were more likely to occur when smoking was permitted, when cigarettes were easily available and in the presence of other smokers" (p. 64, Shiffman et. al., 1996).
3. Severity Minimization- It's the least on the severity continuum (above) and "It's not illegal". You can get arrested for drinking or drugging and driving but you can't get arrested for overeating and driving. We have a highway patrol and drug court but there is no buffet patrol and the only food court that exists is in the Mall.

In Social Responsibility Therapy, harmful behavior relates to a lack of social responsibility which is the result of a pathological level of social-emotional immaturity. Thus, a very basic summary of Social Responsibility Therapy is an intervention which develops honesty, trust, loyalty, concern and responsibility as competing factors against sexual abuse, physical abuse, property abuse, substance abuse and trust abuse. The main focus of Social Responsibility Therapy is on whether the action being considered is helpful or harmful to self or others. If it is helpful to self and others it is socially responsible and needs to be reinforced. If it is harmful to self and others it is socially irresponsible and needs to be re-directed. Three important treatment goals in Social Responsibility Therapy are to:

1. **Stop the harmful behavior-** Develop the healthy behavior success skills (p. 19- 27) needed to keep from repeating unhealthy, harmful behavior;
2. **Understand the harmful behavior-** Develop awareness of how the unhealthy, harmful behavior was acquired, maintained and generalized to other problem areas and;
3. **Demonstrate helpful behavior-** Develop the healthy relationship success skills (p. 17- 18) needed for positive social adjustment.

The focus of this workbook is on understanding unhealthy, harmful behavior and it is structured to help you discover how that behavior was acquired. The healthy behavior success skills you need to keep from repeating the problem (i.e., **A**void trouble; **C**alm down; **T**hink it through and; **S**olve the problem) are integrated into each workbook section. Developing healthy relationship success skills through honesty, trust, loyalty, concern and responsibility is also included.

Introspection 101: Becoming a Careful Self-Observer

Introspection means looking inside of yourself at your motivations for what you do which is the key to developing self-awareness. Becoming a careful observer of others and pointing out their problems is easy but you have to train yourself to look at your problem thoughts, feelings and motivations. Social Responsibility Therapy uses a Structured Discovery approach to help you look at yourself through *structured* exercises that help you *discover* important thoughts and feelings that are connected to unhealthy, harmful behavior. This process increases your self-awareness which develops your self-efficacy (confidence) and helps you maintain your self-control responsibility. Self-control is needed to achieve your personal goals and maintain successful relationships. The social responsibility of self-control tends to get overlooked in our school systems which teach effective control of baseballs, basketballs and footballs but leave it up to you to develop effective control of thoughts, feelings and behaviors.

Developing self-awareness through the structured discovery exercises in this workbook is like playing cards. Each section represents a hand of cards with different statements that may apply to you. Your job is to get honest with yourself by carefully looking at each statement for connections between that information and your behavior (like drawing a new card to see if it can be used in your hand). If the statement applies to you or adds to your understanding of yourself, mark it, if not let it go (discard) and move on to the next piece of information to consider (draw another card). Having the courage to accept the workbook statements that apply to you will allow you to put together a winning hand of connections between thoughts, feelings and motivations.

These connections will provide you with an understanding of how you got involved with your unhealthy, harmful behavior. If you are a mental health professional and are reviewing this workbook for use with your clients, information is provided for you in Appendix A (page 107).

There are two basic things that you can't change in life, the past and other people's behavior. As mentioned earlier, it has been said that "If you're not working on the solution, you're part of the problem". This is the case with many individuals with unhealthy, harmful behavior whose energy is too focused on the past and other people's behavior. Individuals who have problems with unhealthy, harmful behavior tend to spend far too much time ruminating (i.e., going over and over) on past injustices done to them by others, trying to cover up past mistakes of their own and trying to influence other people's opinions of them. This negative coping style maintains unhealthy pride, diverts energy away from solving your harmful behavior problem and makes you feel helpless since you can't change the past or other people's behavior.

In Social Responsibility Therapy, the focus is on the present and your behavior. While it is true that you can't change the past, you can change your honesty about it and understanding of it. Working on your honesty, trust, loyalty, concern and responsibility (which includes self-control) develops healthy pride and dignity. Understanding how you got this problem and learning the healthy behavior success skills to manage it are the first steps toward positive change. In order to successfully complete this workbook, you need to be willing to "set your pride aside" and use this workbook as a mirror to see yourself by carefully considering each statement. This begins with getting honest about past behavior that has been unhealthy to you or harmful to others.

History of Unhealthy, Harmful Behavior
"The more extensive a man's knowledge of what has been done,
the greater will be his power of knowing what to do" -- Benjamin Disraeli (1804-1881)

Record the Type, Duration, Frequency, Severity and Impact on Others
Why go back through the past? That was then, this is now. What's in it for me to go through this again, other than bringing up bad memories? The answer is simple, to learn enough about the past to prevent your past history from repeating itself. In order to prevent history from repeating itself, you have to study history to make yourself aware of the problems and traps to avoid.

Circle all of the forms of harmful behavior on the Harmful Behavior Continuum (Table 1, p. 2) that you have ever been involved with in your life. Then complete the basic information about yourself below and then begin yourself understanding work.

Name: _____   **Date:** _____

Date of Birth: _____   Sex: _____   Race: _____

Education: _____   Occupation: _____   Marital Status: _____

Referral problem (What harmful behavior resulted in your referral for treatment or caused you to get this workbook?): _____

Name of your current treatment program or provider: _____

Your current treatment Setting: __ Outpatient; __ Intensive Outpatient; __ Residential/Inpatient; __ Secure Residential/Correctional Facility; __ Self-help, not in treatment

Check all of the types of harmful behavior you have done. Then underline the parts that apply to you.

____ Trust abuse- For example, lying, cheating, conning, coercion, fraud, running away, child neglect, walking out on a friend in need, shifting loyalties to others when it benefits you or when things aren't going well for current friends, using people for what they have, saying "I love (or really care about) you" just to get sex or justify having it. Making false allegations or filing false charges. Problem priorities- for example: Parents putting involvement in relationships before family/child care (see Planning Problems, p. 122); Putting negative associates before positive friends/family; Doing too much work and forgetting about relationships or getting too involved in relationships and forgetting about responsibilities; Putting other life tasks or relationships before treatment. Doing too much for others and not caring for yourself or getting too caught up in your problems and forgetting about others.

____ Responsibility neglect- Letting your responsibilities go and just doing what you want, what is easiest, what you feel like doing or what makes you feel good at the time. Putting off responsibilities until someone else does them, making excuses to avoid doing things you just don't want to do, Youth example- making excuses to miss or skip school/work, not completing activities that are required of you. Adult example- failure to pay bills or being an absent parent to your children (see Planning Problems, p. 122).

____ Responsibility abuse- Refusal to accept responsibilities. Examples include quitting school or job training, quitting a job without getting another job first, defaulting on loans, not paying people back, not paying child support, using "survival" as an excuse for drug dealing addiction to "easy money", using not being able to find a job that pays enough as an excuse to live off of others without working at all. Cover-up for others abuse, not saying anything.

____ Responsibility overdose- Over-involvement in work/workaholic and neglecting relationships or family. Falling into becoming responsible for everyone and everything all the time, resulting in others always calling on you to get things done or help them out and not taking time to care for yourself (see Need Problems, p. 122).

____ Food abuse (i.e., overeating/overweight, excessive eating/binging, purging or starving self)

____ Substance abuse- legal substances (e.g., alcohol, prescription medications, cigarettes/tobacco or other legal substances- List here _____).

____ Substance abuse- illegal substances (e.g., marijuana, cocaine, methamphetamine, heroin or other recreational/street drugs- List here _____).

____ Property abuse- legal activity including money abuse (e.g., credit card debt, excessive borrowing, gambling debt, compulsive gambling, overspending or shopaholic)

____ Property abuse- illegal activity (e.g., theft, vandalism, arson, forgery, black mail or extortion/getting money by threats, or other property abuse- List here _____).

___ Physical abuse- harm to self (e.g., cutting self, pulling hair out, excessive scratching, picking skin off, injury from banging head or punching walls, suicide attempt)

___ Physical abuse- harm to others (e.g., assault, domestic violence, robbery, kidnapping, school bullying, physical intimidation, child physical abuse/excessive physical punishment)

___ Sexual abuse- harm to self or others (e.g., rape, child sexual abuse/molestation, sexual harassment, exhibitionism/flashing, voyeurism/peeping, prostitution, pandering/pimping, excessive/compulsive sexual behavior including cruising for sex, promiscuity, affairs, pornography, deviant masturbation, dangerous sex, unprotected sex with people I just met)

___ Other problem behavior (list-_____)

Referral Behavior History- Use the space below to write a history of the harmful behaviors and events that resulted in your referral for treatment, got you thinking you need to change or resulted in someone close to you telling you that you need to change. Include: **who** (your behavior hurt, self, others, both, be specific, give names); **what** (your referral behavior was, the primary reason you were referred for or need treatment); **when** (you started it and how long it has gone on); **where** (you usually did it or where it occurs often) and; **why** (you think you did it, include anything you can think of that can start it).

Who: _____
_____
_____

What: _____
_____
_____
_____

When: _____
_____
_____

Where: _____
_____
_____

Why: _____
_____
_____
_____

Introduction to The Problem Development Triad
"The power of man has grown in every sphere, except over himself"
-- Sir Winston Churchill (1874- 1965)

Some individuals with unhealthy, harmful behavior have never had a reasonable period of abstinence or time in their life where they were free of harmful behavior. They were unable to successfully control their behavior because they never understood:
1. **How they got the problem** to begin with;
2. **Why they kept it up** and;
3. **How it spread** into other types of abuse.

The Problem Development Triad components covered in this three workbook series will be used to help you understand the:
1. **Risk Factor Chain** that led to acquiring your harmful behavior- How you got the problem;
2. **Stress-Relapse Cycle** that maintained it- Why you kept it up once you started and;
3. **Harmful Behavior Anatomy** of factors that generalized it- How it spread to other types.

When you have finished the material needed to complete the summary worksheet at the end of each workbook you will have a graphic representation of how you got your problem (workbook 1), kept it (workbook 2) and spread it to other problem areas (workbook3). A summary of "The Problem Development Triad" used in Social Responsibility Therapy is provided in Figure 1. In Social Responsibility Therapy, our number one responsibility as human beings is self-control. Learning to control unhealthy, harmful behavior is the first and most important step toward getting what you want in life. In the words of Dr. Albert Ellis "We are all fallible human beings" so having serious problems is not the issue. The issue is developing enough:
1. **social maturity** to hold yourself accountable about problems when mistakes are made and reclaim your dignity through honesty (see Healthy Relationship Success Skills, p. 17- 18);
2. **emotional maturity** to learn from life mistakes by becoming aware of the high risk situations that trigger those mistakes (see High Risk Situation Avoidance, p. 19) and;
3. **appropriate social behavior control** to stop unhealthy, harmful behavior using the Healthy Behavior Success Skills (see p. 19- 27).

Crossroads- Life always has important crossroads and the path we choose determines the way our life will turn out. The crossroad in harmful behavior development is at the end of the Risk Factor Chain when you first started your harmful behavior. The Risk Factor Chain sets you up for harmful behavior and can lead to a number of types of interpersonal abuse (e.g., physical, verbal, sexual or trust abuse) or substance abuse (e.g., drugs, alcohol, cigarettes or food abuse). If an individual has enough risk factors in each link of the Risk Factor Chain to lead them into a harmful behavior, their use of positive or negative coping determines what happens next.

The Awareness Training goal at the end of this workbook is for you to understand your cycle with enough confidence to be able to explain it clearly to others. In order to reach this level of understanding you will need to complete each of the five phases in "The Stress-Relapse Cycle" and be able to give at least one specific example of a healthy behavior success skill that you have used to address each personal risk factor. If you are able to understand and address these factors,

Figure 1. The Problem Development Triad
(Managing these risk, stress and generalization problems is summarized in Exhibits 1-3, p. 104)

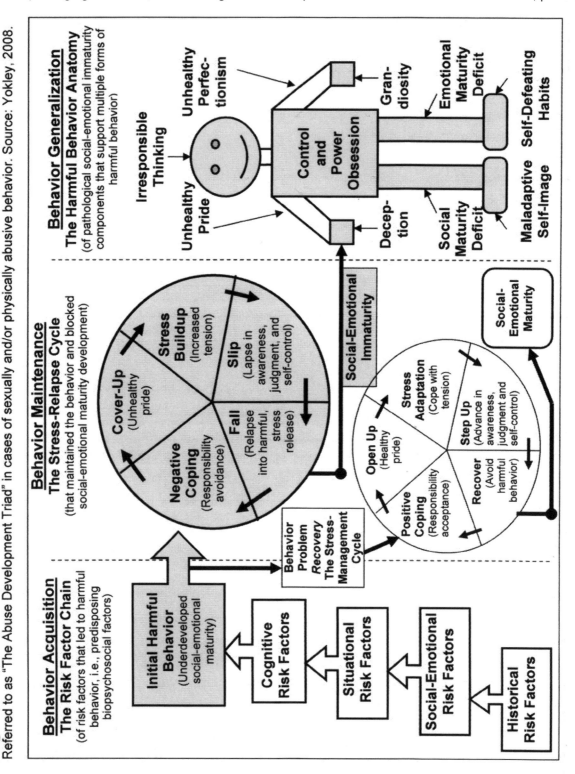

Figure 1. The Problem Development Triad: How Harmful Behavior Was Acquired, Maintained & Generalized. Referred to as "The Abuse Development Triad" in cases of sexually and/or physically abusive behavior. Source: Yokley, 2008.

you will have successfully decreased your relapse risk in addition to developing your confidence in managing your present problem.

Using positive coping is the more difficult path to take after a period of harmful behavior because admitting the problem can result in unwanted consequences. However, positive coping has the added advantages of:

- Developing **honesty** and letting go of unhealthy pride that makes it worse by covering up;
- Repairing broken **trust** and developing the positive relationships needed to stay on track;
- Reducing stress-build up from anxiety about getting caught or guilt about what you did by doing the right thing and being **loyal** to family values (what is right for yourself and others);
- Showing **concern** for yourself and others by keeping your problem up front and thinking ahead about the consequences of falling back into secret-keeping;
- Developing **responsibility** by holding yourself accountable and learning to solve problems by focusing on the present and your behavior, not the past and other people's behavior.

In summary, the drawbacks of positive coping are the consequences of honesty. Although "honesty has its price, the good news is that you don't have to pay twice". The advantages of positive coping include adapting to the stress of making mistakes by reclaiming your dignity through your honesty, trust, loyalty and responsibility. Positive coping leads to resilience (bouncing back) by learning from experience which develops social maturity and wisdom (see Figure 2). During the course of this workbook, you will develop your positive coping skills using the Situation Response Analysis Log in Appendix D (p. 127). Exhibits 1, 2 and 3 (p. 104- 106) provide positive coping summaries of for risk factor management, stress management and management of factors that support multiple forms of harmful behavior.

Figure 2.   The Prevention or Development of Harmful Behavior

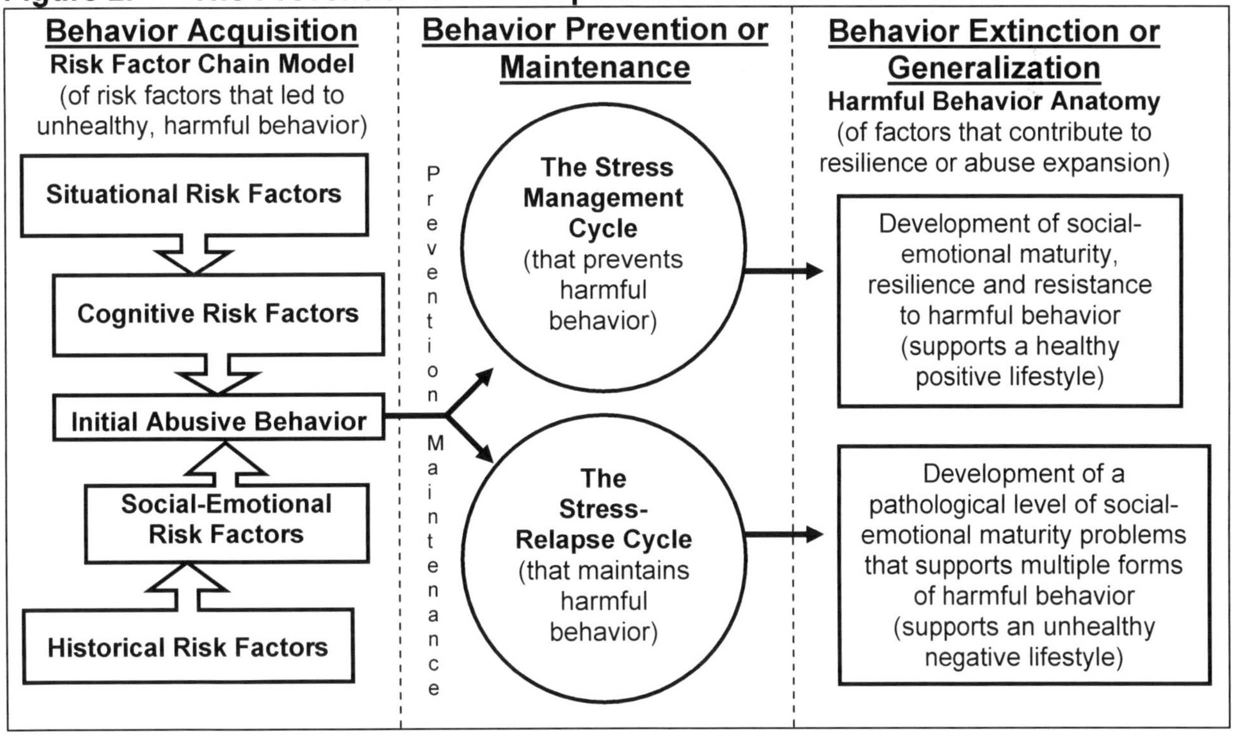

Using negative coping, denying the problem, and covering it up by "acting as if" everything is alright, avoids dealing with the problem. Negative coping creates stress build-up. This eventually results in slipping up and taking a fall back into the Stress-Relapse Cycle that maintains unhealthy, harmful behavior (Figure 2, p. 9). Falling back into the cycle reinforces the social-emotional maturity problems that prevent learning from experience and supports multiple forms of harmful behavior that result in an unhealthy, unhappy, negative life. Over time, repeated relapse through the Stress-Relapse Cycle develops a level of social-emotional maturity problems that spreads one type of unhealthy, harmful behavior to other types or other areas of your life. Given this situation, the harmful behavior that brought you to treatment is often not your only harmful behavior. Also, the harmful behavior that resulted in your referral for treatment may not be the first harmful behavior that you developed. Examples include earlier alcohol abuse being in remission (now under control) but getting substituted with urges to take out feelings on others verbally and physically (i.e., the "dry drunk" syndrome). Earlier trust abuse (i.e., abusing the trust of others by lying, cheating, manipulating, conning, etc.) may go into remission (increasing boredom) but the excitement of trust abuse can get substituted by cocaine abuse. Perhaps excessive or risky sexual behavior is in remission but the untreated emotional maturity problem of self-control is now showing itself through excessive eating or risking money (gambling). Or maybe unhealthy overeating is in remission but is now being substituted with over-spending.

"Knowledge is power." The more we know about how we developed our present behavior patterns, what maintained that behavior and how it spread to other areas, the more confident we can be in understanding ourselves, understanding others, maintaining positive behavior change and achieving positive life goals. It takes a great deal of work to get a clear understanding of your unhealthy, harmful behavior. Not everyone will succeed. To achieve a positive lifestyle, developing self-understanding must include developing dignity through honesty, trust, loyalty, concern and responsibility. Not everyone will continue on the path to social responsibility. Those that do will develop the self-understanding that builds the self-confidence needed for self-control of unhealthy, harmful behavior and maintenance of a healthy, positive lifestyle.

Getting what we want in life

Getting what we want in life involves becoming who we want to be. "Who do we want to be?" can be a difficult question. Who we are is easy to answer and summarized in Table 2 below. According to the ancient Greek philosopher Aristotle (384 BC-322 BC), "We are what we repeatedly do".

Table 2. Who we are According to Aristotle

According to Aristotle…	On the other hand…
• If we repeatedly lie, we are a liar • If we repeatedly drink, we are a drunk • If we repeatedly steal, we are a thief • If we repeatedly beat people, we are a bully • If we repeatedly sexually abuse, we are a sex abuser • If we repeatedly commit crimes, we are a criminal	• If we are repeatedly honest, we are trustworthy • If we are repeatedly trustworthy, we are loyal. • If we are repeatedly loyal, we care • If we are repeatedly care, we are responsible

"Who do we want to be?" is a difficult question that gets people side tracked on <u>external characteristics</u> such as fortune, fame, beauty, brilliance and power. All of these external characteristics require one thing- other people acknowledging, admiring and appreciating them. An easy exercise to help us re-focus on important <u>internal characteristics</u> that we want to have is to simply to look at what we want from others.

What do we want from others? Table 3 below is a survey of over 100 groups of foster parents and youth who were asked… "If you were able to get online at www.godgiveme.com and select the ideal best friend, close family member and life partner (girlfriend, boyfriend, husband or wife), what characteristics would you want that person to have?"

Table 3. Summary of What We Want from Others
(i.e., What Youth, Parents, and Treatment Staff Want from Best friends, Close Family and Life Partners)

Honesty	Trust	Loyalty	Concern	Responsibility
Honest	Trustworthy	Loyal	Caring	Responsible
Assertive,	Obedient	Dependable	Loving	Financially stable
Expressive	Gives you	Sharing	Understanding	Good money
Truthful	space, not nosy	Faithful	Kindness	management
	Reliable	Not a	Nurturing	Respectful
	Not jealous	backstabber	Supportive	Neat, clean, and
	Not possessive	Not a gossip	Considerate	tidy
	Not	Not promiscuous	Nice	Sober, drug free
	overprotective	Not a prostitute	Pleasant	Helpful
		Doesn't cheat	Give and take	Socially mature
			Not selfish	Good morals
			Sensitive	Common sense
			Good listener	Role model
			Tolerant	Reliable
			Open-minded	Good hygiene
			Unconditional	Helps discipline
			love	Has life goals,
				College plans, a
				goal setter
				Self-control
				Work ethic,
				achiever,
				Employed, self-
				motivated
				Punctual, stays
				organized

Source: Reprinted with permission from Table 3.7 (Yokley, 2008).

The results were overwhelmingly consistent in revealing that both youth and adults alike want honesty, trust, loyalty, concern and responsibility in their best friends, close family members and life partners (girlfriend, boyfriend, husband or wife). This begs the question, "If honesty, trust, loyalty, concern and responsibility is what we want from other people in our life, what do we think they want from us?" The bottom line conclusion here is simple, since you can't get any of these things without giving them, if we want honesty, trust, loyalty, concern and responsibility from others, then this is what we should we be trying to develop in ourselves. That's very easy to say and very hard to do, because each of these things has consequences and takes both courage and good judgment to manage well. For example, while it is true that "the truth will set you free" (of guilt and worry about getting caught), the tremendous consequences that come with honesty is why we value it so much. Anyone who has been betrayed, played or back stabbed knows that trust and loyalty can be risky, takes courage and requires good judgment about who can be trusted and who to give your loyalty to. On the other side of the coin, if you are not trustworthy and are disloyal, you will eventually find yourself by yourself, without friends or the support from others needed to help maintain a positive healthy life. Concern and responsibility are also things that you have to learn to manage well. Caring too much about others who are not doing the right thing for themselves, eventually leaves you disappointed and depressed while not caring enough leaves you disconnected and deprived of healthy positive relationships. Likewise, being too responsible and doing too much for others, eventually leaves you resentful of having to carry their weight but not being responsible enough gets you resented by others who have to carry your weight, leaves you unemployed and unwanted by employers.

Getting what we want in life

Getting what we want in life involves breaking the stress-relapse cycle of harmful behavior that develops social maturity problems and going to the opposite extreme by acting honest, trustworthy, loyal, concerned and responsible. This means learning to "act as if" [2] we are who we want to be and practicing that behavior until it becomes automatic. Let's break this down and clear up "what's in it for me" to be honest, trustworthy, loyal, concerned and responsible. When it comes to honesty, the first thing that comes to most people's minds is that honesty brings consequences. If we are standing in front of the judge when they ask "How do you plead?" and answer, "Guilty your honor", we know that our honesty will bring consequences. So here's the drill, we need to accept that the reason people value honesty so much is the tremendous consequences attached to it. If it were easy and carried no consequences, everybody would be honest all of the time. We have to get real with ourselves, admit that we look up to people who are honest, not only because we can trust what they say but because. "Honesty has its price, the good news is you don't have to pay twice". On the flip side of honesty, "dishonesty is disrespect". The people who lie to you are disrespecting you by treating you like a know nothing chump who will never figure it out or a nobody who just doesn't deserve the truth. If you keep disrespecting people by being dishonest, you lose every friend who values honesty and end up surrounded by liars who disrespect you through their dishonesty.

Let's move on to trust. A socially immature belief about trust is that getting respect has more to do with being tough than being trustworthy. Let's think that one through. In life it's win some, lose some, you can't win all the card games, arguments or fist fights. Since socially immature people don't know the difference between disrespect, disagreement, respect and fear. They mistake disagreement for disrespect and mistake fear for respect. As a result, they turn a disagreement with you into a fistfight if they can't change your mind and view using fear to get agreement as getting respect. Be honest, in this situation, when they are walking away running their mouth about you what are you really thinking? Do you really tell yourself, "I really respect that person and want to be more like them?" or are you really thinking, "What an immature a##hole" when they pull that baby crap. So here's a question you have to get honest with yourself about… Can people demand your respect by bullying you or do they have to earn your respect by being trustworthy? The really good news here is that you don't have to trust people to be trustworthy; all you have to do is what you say you will do.

In the area of loyalty, without going into great detail, relationship disloyalty is just too dangerous to put up with in today's HIV world. Picking looks over loyalty has always resulted in emotional heartbreak but now the penalty for that decision can be a premature death. In the area of family loyalty picking negative peers over positive family may help you hear what you want but it prevents you from hearing the truth from positive people who have your best interests in mind. Getting relationship opinions from positive people who have your bests interests in mind is very important because, not being loyal enough to positive people can but you just far behind in life and being too loyal to negative people can put you in the hospital or behind bars.

With respect to concern, we need a healthy balance. Socially immature people tend to go too far in both directions with concern. Some spend too much time following their need for acceptance, doing for others and putting more into relationships than they get out. Picking companionship over concern and compromising themselves to be accepted in unhealthy or abusive relationships does eliminate loneliness and guarantees companionship but results in resentment for putting in too much or regret for bringing on unwanted emotional drama and physical trauma. On the flip side, others spend too much time following their needs for attention or excitement, doing what they want, when they want for the reason they want and taking much more from relationships than they put in. These "take-aholics" don't consider the impact of their selfish behavior on others, focusing only on, "You got to look out for number one". The socially mature balancing act here involves being able to accept that, "You're number one but there are other numbers" and take good care of yourself so you can take good care of those you care about most.

Responsibility does not mean having a great job like owning your own company or having an important title like attorney, doctor or president. Responsibility means that you can be counted on to finish what you start and to give 100% of your ability to your obligations, whether that involves building houses or taking care of your household. Responsible people are people who can be counted on, they are the "go to" people you call when you need something done well.

The bottom line here is simple, when you call someone "immature" you are almost always referring to problems with social maturity (i.e., honesty, trust, loyalty, concern or responsibility) and when grandma told us to "just grow up", she meant to let go of our social immaturity and start acting honest, trustworthy, loyal, concerned and responsible. Who really wants to be around socially immature people? Social maturity problems interfere with developing a "right living" [3] positive lifestyle (i.e., based on the multicultural prosocial values of honesty, trust, loyalty, concern and responsibility) and prevents us from having a healthy, positive life with healthy, positive relationships. Even if you tell yourself that developing a "right living" positive lifestyle by being honest, trustworthy, loyal, concerned and responsible is boring, you have to admit that you don't like people who are not that way with you which means, if you want acceptance instead of rejection from others you need to act this way. In the following section, we will be learning about the Stress-Relapse Cycle and how that cycle develops problems with honesty, trust, loyalty, concern and responsibility which we call "social maturity".

Learning about your stress-relapse cycle is very important in recovery from harmful behavior because it clearly illustrates that if we want to have the social maturity that it takes to get what we want in life, we need to break the Stress-Relapse Cycle that is creating problems with our honesty, trust, loyalty, concern and responsibility. Even if in the most extreme case we find someone with no desire to have a positive life with healthy positive relationships who only wants successful business relationships that will bring personal wealth. Breaking the Relapse Cycle and building social maturity still applies. Think about it. How long would you continue to do business with someone who has problems with honesty, trust, loyalty, concern and responsibility? The bottom line here is simple. If you respect someone, you're honest with them. If you respect someone, you can be trusted by them and you trust them. If you respect someone, you're loyal to them. If you respect someone, you're concerned about them. If you respect someone, you're responsible with them.

Best Practice Treatment for Harmful Behavior
The best practice treatment for harmful behavior includes adopting the Therapeutic Community Pendulum Concept(Yokley, 2008) that "you have to go to the opposite extreme in order to meet the median." In the Pendulum Concept values and associated behavior that were allowed to swing way over to the very negative, harmful side before treatment are required to swing way over to the very positive opposite extreme during treatment. This requirement focuses on developing an opposite extreme positive behavior track record during treatment so that after treatment when self-control naturally swings back some, our behavior will still be positive enough to meet the community behavior standard median and we can survive in that setting without relapse. This "over-correction" training approach of consistently "acting as if" [2] we have opposite extreme prosocial values by practicing opposite extreme behaviors during treatment is a therapeutic community training method [4] similar to military boot camp where the physical stamina requirements exceed what may be needed during battle in order to insure that recruits can adjust to the battlefield and survive. In our goals to avoid death on the battlefield and avoid relapse in the community, "Hesitation kills". On the battlefield, hesitation to follow an order kills your ability to survive. In community treatment, hesitation to "act as if" and go to the opposite extreme, kills your ability to recover.

SRT Opposite Extreme Values and Behaviors
In SRT, honesty, trust, loyalty, concern and responsibility are reinforced to prevent harmful behavior because these multicultural prosocial values are the opposite extreme to the antisocial values used in harmful behavior and are not compatible with unhealthy, harmful behavior. For example, it is not possible to be a dishonest, irresponsible drug abuser while being honest and responsible or it is not possible to be a physically abusive cheating boyfriend while being concerned and loyal. In general, it is difficult to go through with harmful behavior while considering the impact of that behavior and "acting as if" by going to the opposite extreme helps break harmful behavior habits. In summary, SRT requires that we "go to the opposite extreme"

of harmful behavior by modeling healthy, helpful behavior which is are not compatible with and thus competes against that harmful behavior. harmful behavior such as trust abuse, substance abuse, property abuse, physical abuse and sexual abuse require us to be dishonest, untrustworthy, disloyal, selfish and irresponsible, going to the opposite extreme and acting honest, trustworthy, loyal, concerned and responsible act as "blockers" to these harmful behaviors. Opposite extreme values are associated with opposite extreme behaviors used to help you break each phase of the stress-relapse cycle.[4] This is summarized in Table 4 below.

Table 4.
SRT Opposite Extreme Values and Behaviors

Negative Behavior Phases in the Stress-Relapse Cycle	Opposite Extreme Positive Behavior Phases in the Stress-Management Cycle
Negative coping- not accepting responsibility, dishonesty about problems (An honesty problem- denial to self)	**Positive coping**- accepting responsibility, honesty about problems, "To thine own self be true". Get honest with yourself
Cover up of problems to avoid consequences, unhealthy pride, untrustworthy (A trust problem- deception, lying to others, holding negative contracts)	**Open up** about problems, accept consequences, use healthy pride to hold self accountable "The truth will set you free" and hold others accountable, "Be your brother's keeper". Rebuild trust by getting honest with others.
Stress buildup- increased tension from not being loyal to what you know is right and who is right, cover up stress (A loyalty problem)	**Stress adaptation**- cope with tension by being loyal to what you know is right and who is right.
Slip- sliding back in awareness, judgment or self-control (A concern problem- about self not keeping problem "up front" and others not considering the impact of harmful behavior on others)	**Step Up** in awareness, judgment and self-control, show concern for self by keeping you problem "up front" and for others by putting yourself in their shoes, thinking about the impact of your behavior.
Fall- relapse into harmful behavior, not protecting the welfare of self and others (A responsibility problem- "Our #1 responsibility is self-control")	**Recover**- Avoid or escape relapse. Be responsible by maintaining self-control in order to protect the welfare of self and pothers.

In order to help prevent harmful behavior relapse, SRT also sets opposite extreme positive rules [4] to prevent harmful behavior relapse based on the logic that setting the bar high opposite extreme moves a behavior slip (lapse) further away from a behavior fall (relapse). Put another way, "If you aim for the stars, you may hit the trees and if you aim for the trees you may hit the ground".[5] Examples of SRT opposite extreme positive treatment rules are provided in Table 5.

Table 5.
SRT Opposite Extreme Positive Rules

Harmful Behavior	Relapse Triggers
Sexual abuse	No pornography
Physical abuse	No threats or cursing others
Property abuse	No borrowing
Substance abuse	No cigarettes
Trust abuse	No excuses

SRT Opposite Extreme Healthy Behavior Success Skills

Opposite extreme healthy behavior success skills[4] are used to maintain opposite extreme positive rules and behaviors which are required to maintain our number one responsibility of self-control and avoid relapse. Opposite extreme healthy behavior success skills help counter the negative dysfunctional family law that, "What I want to do is right and the reason its right is because I want to do it" associated with harmful behavior. Understanding each SRT healthy behavior success skill involves a simple learning experience broken down into Awareness training, Responsibility training and Tolerance training. In life "talk is cheap" and your "ACTS speak louder that your words". In SRT, your number one responsibility is self-control and your responsible ACTS are to: Avoid trouble; Calm down; Think it though and; Solve the problem. The ACTS healthy behavior success skills are outlined in Table 6.

Table 6. Opposite Extreme Healthy Behavior Success Skills

Harmful Behavior Stance	Opposite Extreme "ACTS"
Never back down, Stand your ground, Divide and conquer	**Avoid Trouble** (Relapse prevention)
Create chaos, Stir it up, Get worked up, Stay worked up, Work others up	**Calm Down** (Emotional regulation)
Go with your gut Act on impulse	**Think it through** (Decisional balance)
Forget fighting it, do what you want. Don't work it out, block it out. "That was then, this is now"	**Solve the problem** (Social problem solving)

Cycles, Cycles and More Cycles

Stress-relapse cycles are have been observed across a number of harmful behaviors. For example: the substance abuse relapse-recovery cycle (Scott, Dennis and Foss, 2005); the physical abuse cycle of violence (Dutton, 2007); the sexual abuse maintenance cycle (Kahn, 1996); the unhealthy eating binge-diet cycle (Schulherr, 1998; 2005) and; the gambling cycle (Nower and Blaszczynski, 2006). With respect to harmful emotions an anger-relapse cycle (Clancy, 1996; 1997) and depression-rumination cycle (Law, 2005; Nolen-Hoeksema and Davis, 1999) have been described. The point is this, harmful behavior habits are repeating cycles that humans fall into and need to learn to break.

The Crossroads after harmful behavior episode:
Positive vs Negative Coping, Recovery or Relapse?

After committing an unhealthy, harmful behavior, if you use positive coping, accept and work on the problem, don't make excuses and get honest, two things are likely. First, you are likely to get help to avoid doing it again and second there is likely to be consequences. In short, "Honesty

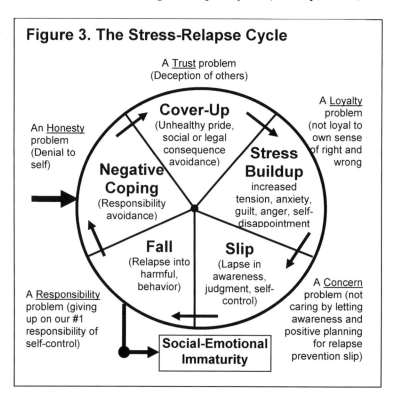

Figure 3. The Stress-Relapse Cycle

has its price but the good news is you don't have to pay twice". If you use negative coping, you are likely to fall into the Stress Relapse Cycle that maintains harmful behavior.

The Stress-Relapse Cycle
"We are what we repeatedly do"- Aristotle (384 BC-322 BC)

The Stress-Relapse Cycle plays an important part in relapse prevention because it: 1) describes the cycle that maintains harmful behavior; 2) summarizes the basic factors in each phase of the cycle that increase relapse risk and; 3) provides the skills needed in each phase to break the Stress-Relapse Cycle. A Stress-Relapse Cycle summary is provided in Figure 3.

Breaking the Stress-Relapse Cycle
Breaking the Stress-Relapse Cycle involves being able to answer the following five basic relapse cycle questions in order to make a relapse prevention plan that works for you.

Making a Relapse Prevention Plan that Works for You:
Five Relapse Cycle Questions to Answer
1. After making a mistake and falling back into your harmful behavior, what did you tell yourself to deal with it?
2. What did you do to keep your harmful behavior from being detected?
3. What stressful thoughts, feelings and situations are you experiencing?
4. What slips have you noticed that can lead you to fall back into your harmful behavior?
5. What do you believe led you to fall back into your harmful behavior this last time?

Since these questions are easy to ask but hard to answer, the rest of this workbook is structured to help you discover the answers that fit your specific situation and how to use the ACTS healthy behavior success skills to develop a Stress-Management Cycle (Figure 1) that works for you.

Summary of Healthy Relationship and Behavior Success Skills
The awareness training focus of this workbook is on helping you understand how your unhealthy, harmful behavior was maintained by the Stress-Relapse Cycle. During awareness training on what maintained the problem, it is equally important to keep the problem under control. This requires a responsibility and tolerance training focus on: 1) the healthy behavior success skills needed to change that harmful behavior and; 2) the healthy relationship success skills needed to form a positive support network that will help maintain that positive change.

The healthy behavior success skills you need to keep from falling back into harmful, negative behavior are: **A**void trouble; **C**alm down; **T**hink it through and; **S**olve the problem.[6] The healthy relationship success skills you need for positive relationship development and to help you maintain behavior change are honesty, trust, loyalty, concern and responsibility. In relationships these are the things that we want from others in our life and that others want from us. Both healthy behavior and relationship success skills are needed for positive community adjustment and to get what you want in life. These skills are related to each other and support each other.

Healthy <u>Relationship</u> Success Skills (Description)

Honesty- Involves getting honest with yourself about your mistakes and with others about their mistakes. Tell yourself the truth about the feelings that others could have about your actions and how you feel about the actions of others. Getting honest involves learning to "Calm down" so that you don't justify lying based on fear of consequences (see p. 22- 23) and learning to "Think it through" by weighing out the severity of the consequences to yourself and others on the reality scales (see p. 24- 25). Confront deception (see p. 114) in yourself and others. List the benefits of honesty and how you can improve it. What could you do differently? Get others opinions.

_____

_____

_____

Trust- Involves: 1) <u>building trust</u> in others by taking responsibility to "Avoid trouble" (see p. 19), keeping your word and respecting others feelings along with; 2) <u>learning to trust</u> others by opening up about problems and picking the right people to trust. Avoid trust double standards (see p. 114). List the benefits of trust, how you can improve it, what you can do. Get others opinions.

_____

_____

_____

Loyalty- Involves <u>standing up for what you know is right</u> and who you know is right especially when there is social pressure to keep quiet, i.e., "If you don't stand for something, you'll fall for anything." This means learning to "Think it through" (see p. 24- 25) to avoid Irresponsible Loyalty by going along with what is wrong just to get along, compromising yourself to be accepted or covering up for others (Irresponsible Loyalty, p. 116). List the benefits of loyalty and how you can improve your loyalty below. What could you do differently? Get others opinions.

_____

_____

Concern- Involves: 1) <u>helping self</u> by keeping problems "up front" as a daily priority so that they don't get out of control again; 2) <u>helping others</u> by treating them the way they want to be treated; 3) blocking helplessness by taking responsibility to "Solve the Problem" (see p. 25- 27) instead of blaming others (i.e., "when you blame other people for your behavior, you give them control over your life") and 4) substituting the "Don't care attitude" with the courage to care, share and try (see p. 116- 117). In group and family therapy, use your PRAISE skills (p. 28) to show concern for others. List the benefits of concern, how to improve, what you can do. Get others opinions.

_____

_____

Responsibility- <u>Our number one responsibility is self-control</u> which involves learning to: **A**void trouble; **C**alm down; **T**hink it through and; **S**olve the problem (see p. 24- 25). Other important responsibilities are making things right (emotional restitution), pulling our own weight and learning to accept feedback. Getting what we want in life requires awareness of Responsibility Issues (see p. 117). List responsibility benefits, how to improve, what you can do. Get others opinions.

_____

_____

_____

Healthy <u>Behavior</u> Success Skills (Instructions)

Let's face it, most people who are completing a harmful behavior workbook at one point in their lives have been told to avoid trouble, calm down, think things through before acting or that they need to solve their problem. This was telling you what you already know, not what you really need to know. Everybody knows that what you do matters more than what you say. Grandma probably told you your **ACTS** speak louder than your words. What you really need to know is "how to" **A**void trouble, **C**alm down, **T**hink it through and **S**olve the problem.[6]

How to **A**void trouble: Two Basic Skills

If you have had some treatment experience in the past, you may have heard the skills used to avoid trouble referred to as "relapse prevention". These skills basically involve becoming aware of your high risk situations for relapse into unhealthy, harmful behavior and then making relapse prevention plans to avoid or escape those situations. A high risk situation is a person, place or thing (often a thought or feeling) that sets the occasion for falling back into trouble (i.e., harmful behavior). In order to avoid trouble (relapse) you need to know how to deal with high risk situations. Dealing with high risk situations takes two basic types of skills. You need avoidance skills to help you identify high risk situations so you can get around them and you need escape skills to get out of high risk situations when you fall into them or when they find you. The focus in this workbook will be on learning to "Avoid Trouble" by learning high risk situation avoidance and escape skills.

High Risk Situation Avoidance- Use positive planning and fantasy fast forward (p. 113) to avoid trouble. Since it's always easier to avoid trouble (high risk situations) than escape it once started, "If you fail to plan, you plan to fail". Use Positive Planning to avoid high risk situations. Know your high risk situations. Make a list with a positive plan for each high risk person, place or thing/emotion that could lead you back into harmful behavior trouble. "Keep your problem up front", don't let your recovery planning guard down by and put a HALT on falling into high risk situations by not letting yourself get to Hungry, Angry, Lonely or Tired. Think about your last harmful behavior problem and list who you were with, where you were, what you were thinking and feeling at the time. Then list how these people, places and things set the occasion for trouble.

Referral problem- Harmful behavior that resulted in your treatment referral _____

High risk people- Who you were with and how they helped lead you into your referral problem?

_____

Positive plan (to avoid these people)- _____

_____

High risk places- Where were you and how that helped lead you into your referral problem?

_____

Positive plan (to avoid these places)- _____

_____

High risk things- What you were feeling and how did that lead to your referral problem?

_____

Positive plan (to deal with these feelings)- _____

_____

What you were thinking and how did that lead to your referral problem? _____

_____

Positive plan (to manage these thoughts)- _____

_____

> **Hint:** If you are not sure about your thinking, review the irresponsible thinking that can lead to trouble in Appendix C. This may help you become aware of your high risk thoughts that led to trouble.

Avoiding foresight slips into high risk situations- In reality, no matter how good our intentions are, if we don't use positive planning, Murphy's Law kicks in and "whatever can go wrong, will go wrong". If we don't stick to our recovery priorities and relapse prevention plan by avoiding high risk situations, using the reality scales to think our decisions through and weigh the possible consequences, we are likely to make a foresight deficit decision and fall back into harmful behavior trouble. Foresight deficit decisions are foresight slips that lead to falling back into harmful behavior from not being aware of high risk situations, not looking ahead and not thinking about what could happen. Foresight deficit decisions can result in relapse on many types of harmful behaviors. The key to avoiding foresight deficit decisions that lead to harmful behavior relapse is developing self-awareness of: 1) high risk situations for relapse and; 2) the irresponsible thinking (see Appendix C, p. 114) that allows you to enter those high risk situations. One simple way to help you avoid foresight deficit decisions is to use Fantasy Fast Forward where you pretend you are actually the main character in a movie and fast forward to the end in order to help you imagine what may go wrong if you stay in your present situation and don't change course. In short, fantasy fast forward involves learning to "Think ahead and plan ahead to get ahead". Then describe a foresight deficit decision that you have made on your referral problem behavior and how you could use fantasy fast forward to avoid the same harmful behavior trouble in the future. Sometimes it's easier if you break your foresight deficit decision down by starting at the end with the problem you fell into and working backwards to look at the situations or events you didn't think ahead about that led to that harmful behavior. Like anything else, fantasy fast forward takes practice. In order to get good at it, you have to look at what you could do different next time.

Foresight deficit decision: I fell into a problem with _____

when I didn't think ahead about what could go wrong from _____

_____

> **Hint:** A review of the foresight deficit decisions examples on page 110 in Appendix B and the description of fantasy fast forward at the end on p. 113 should help you with this assignment.

Fantasy Fast Forward: If I think about being in a similar situation again and fast forward to the end, I need to think ahead about _____

and avoid trouble by _____

High Risk Situation Escape- Use the three-Step Social Responsibility Plan (i.e., get out, get honest and get responsible) to escape trouble. Accept that when it comes to getting out of high risk situations, "hesitation kills recovery". Look at the high risk people, places and things that you listed in the previous section and describe how you could use your Three-step responsibility plan to escape.

1. **Get out** (Remove yourself) Involves getting out of the high risk situation by leaving without hesitation. No one thinks clearly in emotional situations. "You need to be laughing and leaving, not staying and stewing" because the longer you stay in the problem situation, the higher the risk of acting irresponsible. Be prepared to escape trouble by developing "concrete face saving mechanisms" (excuses to leave high risk situations that will work) to have ready if needed. Look at the high risk situations you listed above. What could you do or say to get

   away from these people and out of these places? _____

   _____

2. **Get honest** (Block irresponsible thinking by getting honest with yourself) about: 1) the likelihood of relapse if you return to those high risk situations and block the irresponsible thoughts that "I can handle it, no big deal, nothing will happen", etc. and 2) what will happen to your goals and feelings about yourself if you act on the unhealthy, harmful thoughts that get triggered by high risk people, places or feelings. Use "Fantasy fast forward" to play the tape in your head to the end consequences and tell yourself "I'm not falling into that". Tell yourself the truth that feelings can change over time but once you have done something, that can't be changed. If you can't deny the feeling, delay it by telling yourself "I can always come back here or do this tomorrow". What could happen next if you don't stay out of that

situation and how will you will feel later? _____

_____

Using the reality scales can also help you get honest with yourself about the need to stay or escape your high risk situation (See p. 24- 25). Rate the high risk situations you listed above on the scales below.

   Survival scale- "How necessary for my survival is it for me to stay in this situation?"

   0 = not necessary; 10 = necessary to save my life _____
   Success scale- "How important is it to my success in life for me to stay in this situation?"

   0= not important at all; 10= so important I will never succeed in life without it _____
   Severity scale- "How severe could the consequences be if I leave this situation?"

   0= not severe at all; 10= so severe I can't stand it and will need help to handle it _____

3. **Get responsible** (Substitute more responsible thoughts). Replace the irresponsible thoughts about unhealthy, harmful behavior that (e.g., eating, drinking, drugging, smoking, spending, cheating, hitting, cursing, stealing, molesting, running away) that get triggered by high risk situations with responsible thoughts. Begin by asking yourself, "How will that help me? or Why should I hurt me just because other people or other things hurt me?" Then substitute responsible thoughts. For example, "I need to stay out of that situation", "It's not worth the risk", "I need to put my recovery first" and escape trouble.

   What I need to say to myself _____

   What I need to do _____

How to **C**alm down: Two basic skills.
The healthy behavior success skills used to calm down involves emotional control. These skills are often referred to as "emotional regulation" in treatment manuals. If you were standing next to your best friend when a problem situation hit you, they would show you concern by talking you down, not working you up. Unfortunately, we are not usually standing next to our best friend when problems hit. In these situations we have to learn to talk to ourselves like our own best friend. We have to talk ourselves down, not work ourselves up. The two basic skills emotional regulation skills we have to learn in order to stop acting on our emotions are: 1) Emotional Dissipation- How to let go of unwanted feelings and; 2) Emotional Accommodation- How to hold on to unwanted feelings.

Emotional Dissipation (The ABC's of letting feelings go):
Emotional dissipation involves letting go of belief problems that are working you up. The ABC's of letting feelings go are as follows... **"A"** is the Action that occurred (the problem situation or event); **"B"** is the Belief problem, about the action that works you up and triggers problem feelings or urges (i.e., often contains the word "should" or "must"); **"C"** is Challenging the Belief problem about the action in order to stop following the feeling and let it go.[3] For example: Action that occurred- Supervisor in a hurry raises their voice to you on in front of others; Belief problem- Telling yourself "They should respect me" triggers feeling frustrated and angry. This

can result in having the last word and getting consequences if you can't let the feelings go and keep talking; <u>Challenging the Belief problem</u>- "Where is the evidence that people in a hurry, should slow down and lower their voice, I don't" and "How is me doing the wrong thing going to get them to do the right thing?"

Think about the last time you got really upset and had a relapse urge. Apply the ABC's of letting feelings go to that situation and discuss it with your therapist or group if you are in treatment.

<u>A</u>ction that occurred: _____

<u>B</u>elief problem: _____

_____

<u>C</u>hallenging the belief problem: _____

_____

> **Hint:** You can use the who, what, when, where, how and why that you learned in school for writing a short story to challenge belief problems. "Who could prove that? or "I can't prove that" (Validity challenge) "What if the worst happens?" (Preparation challenge) "When/why should I have known better?" (Self-criticism challenge) "Where is the evidence that...?" (Objective challenge) "Why does it follow that...?" (Philosophical challenge), "How likely is it that the negative outcome will occur? (Probability challenge)

Note: The ABC's of letting feelings go were condensed from Rational Emotive Behavior Therapy.[7]

Emotional Accommodation (The ABC's of holding on to feelings):

Physical accommodation is the hot tub example where you get used to the uncomfortable temperature by making yourself stay in the tub until your body gets used to it (i.e., accommodation). Typically your thoughts stop and all your focus is on the hot water sensation along with the cool air around you. Emotional accommodation is where you get used to the uncomfortable feeling by making yourself stay with it until you get used to it, you stop all your thoughts by focusing on your body sensations and the environment around you. This is similar to the cotton candy experience where it's big, it's blue and it's in your face right up until you take a bite out of it and realize there wasn't that much to it. The ABC's of holding on to feelings is structured to help you discover "the cotton candy effect" of facing unwanted feelings and letting yourself accommodate to them. Remember urges and cravings are feelings too!

"A" is Accept the distressing feeling (urge or craving). Accept that distress and discomfort are a real part of everyone's life that we need to accommodate. Accept the trigger situation. Receive the feeling. Don't avoid it. Don't deny that you're upset. Don't distract yourself with activity, slow down and let yourself feel. Be open to unwanted feelings and opinions. Don't change the subject or block others feedback out. All feelings and all opinions are valid because they are someone's view of the world and we are all allowed to have different views. List a feeling that puts you at risk for relapse and how to accept that feeling. What do you say to yourself and do?

_____

_____

_____

"B" is Begin getting used to the feeling (urge or craving). Give yourself permission to feel. Stay with the feeling. Hold on to it. Don't try to minimize it or rationalize it off. Think of a hot tub, don't get out, let yourself accommodate. Find a quiet place if you can. Accept the fact that feelings can't hurt you, but telling yourself "I can't stand it" triggers reactions that can hurt you. Tell yourself, "I dislike this feeling but I can deal with it and don't have to act it out" or "This feeling is disturbing and disappointing but not dangerous so there is no need to take action". Write how could you begin to get used to that feeling that puts you at risk for relapse.

_____

_____

_____

"C" is Channel the feeling (urge or craving) to the right place at the right time. Tell yourself, "I can always act on my feelings tomorrow" to give yourself time to settle. Use your responsible mind to focus your awareness on your sensations. Let your emotional mind coast to a stop and allow thoughtless peace right now. Continue to be aware of the body sensations associated with the feeling, just notice them, don't attach any thoughts to them, don't fight or struggle with them, just be aware of the sensations and let them be. Stay in the moment. Think of the Chinese finger trap, stop struggling and pulling against the feeling, just let it be so you can get free. Imagine you are surfing a big wave using your breath to steady the surfboard though the peak of the urge as it rises and you are staying with it as it slides all the way into the beach. When you have surfed the urge out and the feeling subsides, channel your energy into a positive future image of yourself as the person you want to be in the place you want to be. Stay with that positive image. If the unwanted feeling/urge was triggered by a problem, describe where you could take that problem.

_____

_____

Note: See Chapter 5 in The Clinician's Guide (p. 103) for more on The ABC's of holding on to feelings.

How to **T**hink it through- If you were ever asked "what were you thinking", chances are that you didn't think your decision through before you took action. Thinking it though by balancing the benefits against the drawbacks before making the decision is referred to as "decisional balance" in treatment manuals. Thinking it through is an important part of learning to talk to yourself like your own best friend. False friends who just want to be popular with everyone or people who want to stir up trouble, tell you what you <u>want to hear</u>. They help you minimize unhealthy, harmful behavior by using the words "just" and "only" (e.g., "It's a <u>only</u> little thing, no big deal" or "We'll <u>just</u> do it this one time"). Best friends are honest with you and tell you what you <u>need to hear</u>, not what you want to hear. If you were standing next to your best friend when you were hit with temptation to do something you shouldn't, they would give you a reality check. Your best friend would tell you that in reality, it's <u>only</u> a little thing if no harm can come to yourself or others and it's never <u>just</u> once. Since your best friend can't always be there to give you a reality check, you have to learn to do this yourself. The _reality check_ and _reality scales_ described below will help you weigh things out during difficult decisions, think it through and guide yourself into responsible action.

Use the Social Responsibility Check (reality check) for on the spot "snap" decisions by asking yourself "Is what I'm thinking about doing helpful or harmful to myself or others?" All decisions that could be harmful to self or others need to be weighted out further on three reality scales, the Survival Scale, the Success Scale and the Severity Scale. The Survival Scale evaluates how necessary for my survival it is to do the behavior being considered on a scale of zero (not necessary at all) to ten (absolutely necessary to save my life). Ask yourself, "How necessary for my survival is it for me to do what I am considering?" "What will happen to my survival if I don't act?" The Success Scale evaluates how important for my success is doing the responsible thing or failing to do it on a scale of zero (not important at all) to ten (so important that it could change the entire course of my life). Ask yourself, "How important is it to my success in life for me to do what I am considering?" "Do I have to do this in order to succeed in life?" The Severity (or Awful) Scale ("Bad Scale" for young children) evaluates how severe the consequences of doing the responsible thing or failing to do it will be on a scale of zero (not severe, awful or bad at all) to ten (so severe that I can't stand it, must avoid it and need help to overcome it). On one side of this scale is the reality of what will likely happen if the harmful behavior is committed. For example, "In the worst case, how severe could the consequences be if I smoked, drank or ate this and do I need to avoid these consequences?", "In the worst case, how severe could the consequences be if I took or smashed this and do I need to avoid these consequences?" or "In the worst case, how severe could the consequences be if I hit or fondled this person and do I need to avoid these consequences?" On the other side of this scale is the reality of what will likely happen if the harmful behavior is not committed. "How severe would the consequences be if I do the right thing and decide not to do this? Could I handle these consequences?" In summary, the severity scale is used to show concern for yourself and others by weighing out the severity of the consequences to yourself and others before taking action. [3]

List a recent decision mistake that you made: _____

_____

Apply the Social Responsibility Check to that decision. My decision was (check one)...
__Helpful to me but harmful to others   __Harmful to me but helpful to others

__Helpful to myself and others   __Harmful to myself and others

List an important life decision that you need to make: _____

_____

Use the Reality Scales to weigh out your decision and discuss this with your therapist or group if you are in treatment.

Survival scale rating ___(0- 10); Success scale rating ___(0- 10); Severity scale rating ___(0- 10)

My decision: _____

_____

How to **S**olve the problem- Life always has problems that kick up feelings and require solutions. Behind every problem there is a goal. Problems are only problems when we are not meeting our goals to get what we want in life. The healthy behavior success skills used to solve the problems we face in life are referred to in treatment manuals as "social problem solving". Being able to "solve the problem" is needed to meet our goals to: get what we want; do as well as we want or; be treated the way we want in life. In order to get what you want in life, you need to get SET for solving problems in three steps: 1) Set your goal; 2) Evaluate your progress and options; 3) Take responsible action.

Set your goal involves getting honest with yourself about your goal. Ask yourself, What is my goal? What do I really want? Get honest about the problem and your real goal. Look at actual problem-solving goals not feelings about the problem. There is a big difference between solving the problem and just venting your feelings. For example, imagine you are a young person in a treatment program and your real goal is independence. You feel held back by adults because you are certain you can make it on your own if they just let you go. They keep reminding you that you haven't finished high school and believe you need more treatment to avoid relapse. You keep getting caught up in arguments over whether or not you can make it on your own.

Evaluate your progress and options. Evaluate your progress by asking yourself, "How well is what I am doing working in getting me what I want?" and "How will things likely to turn out for me if I continue this way?" This requires getting honest with yourself about your progress. For example, admitting that "Arguing over whether I can make it on my own if they just get out of my life is getting caught up in venting feelings, has not changed their minds and is not getting me any closer to actually being out on my own." Evaluate your options- Ask yourself, "What are my options?", "What can I change?", "What really needs to get done?" Make as long of a list as you can, be creative ask others for ideas. List all possible options and choices that could get you to your goal, then write it out for yourself. For example, "To be independent, I need my own place which takes money. My options are stealing, dealing, working going into the military or moving in with someone. I can change getting side-tracked in arguments on whether or not I can make it on my own, start really looking at what independence takes, 'keep my eyes on the prize', and figure out a way to get what I want. If I continue to vent my feelings over feeling held back without making a convincing plan to succeed, nothing will change. If I don't show them I know how to avoid relapse, I won't get out of treatment."

Take responsible action involves taking responsibility to change your method by getting honest with yourself about what needs to change and correcting your course. This involves answering the questions, "What do I need to do differently to reach my goal?", "What is the best way to get what I want?" and "What should I try first?" For example, "I need to do two things differently to reach my goal. First, I need to accept that reaching my goal will take more than just getting other people off my back and moving in with someone who will take care of me is not really making it on my own. In all honesty, I need a good job with health benefits or I need to get into the military. Both of these require graduating from high school and not relapsing back into another treatment program. Second, I need to stop letting my feelings get in the way of my goal to be on my own, stop arguing, start studying and finish treatment. I just got so mad when they told me 'you need to stop breeding and start reading' that I let my feelings get in the way of my goal. The best way to get what I want is to make the best relapse prevention plan I can. What I should try first is increased treatment participation and regular study hours." [3]

List a current problem that you are having: _____
Use the steps above to "solve the problem" and discuss this with your therapist or group if you are in treatment.

Set your goal: _____

Evaluate your progress and options: _____

_____

_____

Take responsible action: _____

_____

_____

You can remember the healthy behavior success skills: **A**void trouble; **C**alm down; **T**hink it through and; **S**olve the problem by remembering that "actions speak louder than words" and thinking about your **ACTS**. Make a healthy relationship and behavior success skills cue card out of Table 7 below and carry it with you as a reminder of the skills you need to practice.

Table 7.
Healthy Behavior Success and Relationship Skills Cue Cards

Keep your Skill Cards with you at all times
"There are two basic types of knowledge in life, Knowing it or knowing where to get it" [8]

Social Responsibility Therapy- Healthy <u>Behavior</u> Success Skills[a]

Getting what we want in life involves learning to...

Avoid trouble (relapse prevention)- Use the 3-step social responsibility plan: <u>Get out</u> (Remove yourself)- "You need to be laughing and leaving, not staying and stewing"; <u>Get honest</u> (Block the thought)- Tell yourself the truth, feelings change but actions can't be changed. If you can't deny the thought delay it. Tell yourself "I can always do this tomorrow". <u>Get Responsible</u>[b] (Substitute a more responsible thought)- Weigh your decision on the "Reality Scales".

Calm down (emotional regulation)- The ABC's of letting feelings go: "A" is the <u>Action that occurred</u>; "B" is the <u>Belief problem</u>, i.e., the word "should" or "must" that is triggering the feeling; "C" is <u>Challenging the Belief problem</u> in order to stop working yourself up, prevent following feelings and let it go.[b] (See Ellis & Bernard, 2006; Ellis & Velten, 1992).

Think it through (decisional balance)- Do a Responsibility Check, ask yourself- "Is what I'm considering helpful or harmful to myself and others?" If harmful or unhealthy[b] use the three <u>Reality Scales</u> (0 to 10 scales):
Survival scale- How important to my survival is it for me to... ? ("Am I safe right now?")
Success scale- How important for my success is it for me to...? ("Will this change my life forever?")
Severity scale (Bad or Awful scale)- How severe would the consequences be if I...?

Solve the problem (social problem solving)- Get <u>SET</u> for solving problems: 1) <u>S</u>et your goal; 2) <u>E</u>valuate your progress and options; 3) <u>T</u>ake responsible action[b]

Table 7. (continued)
Healthy Behavior Success and Relationship Skills Cue Cards

Social Responsibility Therapy- Healthy <u>Relationship</u> Success Skills[c]
What do we want from others in our life and what do they want from us?

Developing the relationships we want in life requires <u>mutual</u>...

Honesty- Involves getting honest <u>with yourself and others</u> by taking responsibility for mistakes along with getting honest about others mistakes to keep them from getting in worse trouble later.

Trust- Involves <u>building trust</u> in others by keeping your word and respecting their feelings along with <u>learning to trust</u> others by opening up about problems and picking the right people to trust.

Loyalty- Involves <u>standing up for what you know is right</u> and who you know is right when there is peer pressure to keep quiet, "If you don't stand for something, you'll fall for anything."

Concern- Involves <u>helping self</u> by keeping personal problems "up front" so they don't get out of control again and <u>helping others</u> by treating others the way they want to be treated.

Responsibility- <u>Our number one responsibility is self-control</u>. Three others are emotional restitution (making things right), pulling our own weight and learning to accept feedback.

Social Responsibility Therapy PRAISE Group <u>Process</u> Skills[d]
Group Participation Motivation Skills
Helping yourself and others get the most out of the group learning experience requires...

Pulling people in-Saying things like, " That's a really good point" (Making them a part/Integration)

Responsible reinforcement- Saying things like, "That took a lot of courage", "I respect your honesty" (reinforcing responsible statements).

Acknowledgement - Saying things like, "An important thing that I got from of what you said was...".

Identification (is an obligation in group)- Saying things like, "I can identify with that", "I can see that", "I can understand that", "Makes sense to me" (recognizing the validity of what others say, identifying with them and validating them).

Social mathematics Saying things like, "You're the third person in here that I've heard say that", "He said that to me also", "A lot of people feel that way/have that view/have had that experience" (Cumulative Identification).

Enabling responsibility- Saying things like, "I've made the same mistake", "I did that too", "when I did that the same thing happened to me" or holding yourself accountable by opening the group on yourself to get honest about a mistake (setting the occasion for honesty & accepting responsibility)

Table 7. Footnotes
a. SRT early stage recovery skills to help stabilize and prevent relapse into unhealthy harmful behavior.
b. Do the responsible thing. "Act as if" you are the person you want to be and go to the opposite healthy, helpful extreme
c. SRT late stage recovery skills to help maintain healthy, helpful behavior.
d. SRT group recovery skills to build unity and enhance motivation for participation.
Note: Page numbers in parentheses are referenced to SRT manual, Yokley (2008)

The Problem Development Triad- Section 2: How Harmful Behavior was Maintained

"We are what we repeatedly do" -- Aristotle (384 BC- 322 BC)

Understanding How Harmful Behavior was Maintained: The Stress-Relapse Cycle

After the first episode of behavior that resulted in your treatment referral, no one sat themselves down and said, "This is the life for me, I need to figure out a way to convince myself to continue this unhealthy, harmful behavior so that I can hurt myself or others to the point where I get in some serious trouble and need treatment". What really happened was that they fell into a Stress-Relapse Cycle. This second workbook in the Social Responsibility Therapy series focuses on developing an understanding how harmful behavior was maintained through the Stress-Relapse Cycle (i.e., Section 2 of Problem Development Triad) which acted to further shape, develop and maintain your harmful behavior after you started it. Briefly, this section deals with the question "Why did I keep it up?" while others who were doing it, grew out of it, got over it, got tired of it and changed or got help.

After a unhealthy, harmful behavior there is a crossroads where you must choose to deal with the situation by using negative coping or positive coping. This choice results in: Covering-up or opening-up; Letting Stress Build-Up or using stress management; Slipping up or stepping up; Falling back into or recovering from your harmful behavior. Thus, whether you use positive or negative coping after a harmful behavior episode determines whether you will avoid or continue problems by entering a Stress-Relapse Cycle. This crossroads is illustrated in the "Behavior Prevention or Maintenance" section of Figure 2.

Those who use Positive Coping skills (e.g., honesty and acceptance of responsibility) to deal with their initial harmful behavior episode, will learn from their mistakes which increases the probability of using positive coping skills in the future to deal with stress and mistakes. In the Stress-Management Cycle, Positive Coping (phase 1) by admission of mistakes or problems (to self and others), allows you to reclaim your dignity through your honesty, Open up (phase 2) and work on a solution (healthy pride). Stress adaptation (phase 3) involves actively working on the solution which decreases frustration and increases self-efficacy (confidence) by learning from mistakes. This leads to taking a personal growth Step Up (phase 4) in self-awareness and self-control that helps you Recover (phase 5) from the urge or temptation to follow your feelings (See "The Stress-Management Cycle" in Figure 1).

In Social Responsibility Therapy, positive coping is the first step in managing to stress. Positive Coping involves holding yourself accountable on a daily basis through structured self-evaluation of responses to problem situations. This type of structured adaptive thinking is referred to as Situation Response Analysis and if you have completed workbook 1, you have already been holding yourself accountable by analyzing your responses to situations on your daily Situation Response Analysis Log (Appendix D).

High risk people. High risk people are people that put you at higher risk for harmful behavior. The first step in managing high risk people is accepting that no one is immune to negative social influence and that negative social influence is a powerful relapse trigger. Complete the following questions about the high risk people in your life.

1. Complete the following about your current social network (i.e., people you are around during the day). Who do you know that has been referred to treatment for the same reason that you have or has the same problems?

   _____

   _____

   _____

   Have you ever got them started doing this behavior? _____

   Have they ever got you started? _____

   Who usually starts it you or them? _____

   Should you continue to associate with these people? Why or Why not? _____

   _____

   _____

2. Think about the <u>unhealthy, harmful behavior that resulted in your referred for treatment</u>. How
   many friends and family have you done that behavior with?

   Who were they? _____

   What did you do? _____

   Who usually got it started? _____

3. Who in your social network got you into <u>any form</u> of unhealthy, harmful behavior, what did they do and what did you do?

   _____

   _____

   _____

4. Who in your social network is a positive influence, has never been involved with your harmful behavior and can be counted on to help you avoid it?

   _____

   _____

   _____

Begin the Structured Day for Positive Behavioral Activation

The Structured Day is a Therapeutic Community tool to help avoid relapse into negative behavior by keeping a daily schedule of positive behavior. Behavioral activation is a treatment tool to decrease unwanted feelings by increasing positive activity. Since the brain is basically a three pound problem solving machine, it is important to keep it focused on solving positive activity problems in the present with our behavior to avoid emotional rumination on past problems and other people's behavior (see p. 78). The best way to do this is planning a Structured Day with responsible positive activities. It's simple, just take a sheet of paper, write Monday-Sunday across the top and 6am- 11pm down the left side (leave 8 hours for sleep). Then plug in your responsible activities and post your responsible day in a place that will remind you of what you need to do next. Keep a copy with you if that helps. Reward yourself every evening. first, check off the responsible things you completed with a red marker. Then do a responsibility inventory of "Three things that went right today and how I made that happen" to give yourself credit. Post your responsible week schedule next to the one you did last week so you can see your responsible activity increasing (i.e., more red checks of responsible things getting done each week). If you are having problems, speak to your therapist and/or treatment group.

Begin using your Situation Response Analysis Log

This is a very important part of increasing your self-awareness of the Irresponsible Thinking that you use on everyday problem situations. Make time to sit down every evening to review your day and record events in your log. The Situation Response Analysis Log and instructions are provided for you in Appendix D. Be sure to make at least one log entry every day as you will be using what you learned from this log in your treatment sessions and later in workbook 3. Use this log as a way to become more aware of your thoughts feelings and behavior in difficult situations. Don't forget to record using your Three Step Social Responsibility Plan (below) when you use it as a Positive Coping response to a problem situation. In addition to holding yourself accountable through self-evaluation on your Situation, Response Analysis Log and in treatment sessions, Social Responsibility Therapy involves the expectation that you will hold yourself accountable socially learning to put yourself in other peoples shoes and see things through their eyes through structured perspective-taking, role reversal and behavior impact knowledge enhancement in order to prepare yourself to offer emotional restitution through harmful behavior explanation, clarification and apology. This type of empathy development in Social Responsibility Therapy is referred to as Emotional Restitution Training (Yokley, 2011) and apology/clarification sessions should only be done with your therapist.

The Three Step Social Responsibility Plan.

It does you no good to develop your self-awareness to the point where you can recognize a high risk situation if you stay in that situation until a relapse is triggered. Whenever you become aware of a high risk situation you need to use your Three Step Social Responsibility Plan to: **Get out** of that risk situation right away; **Get honest** with yourself about the irresponsible thoughts that will lead you back into trouble and; **Get responsible** by substituting responsible thoughts that will lead you out of trouble (see p. 22- 23). Discuss the Three Step Social Responsibility Plan with your therapist or in your treatment group and give examples of how you can apply it to steer clear of several different types of trouble.

Justifying actions based on feelings is an important aspect of irresponsible thinking active in negative coping which leads to falling back into the Stress-Relapse Cycle of unhealthy, harmful behavior. In order to address this problem it is important to: 1) become aware of your basic human emotions (summary below); 2) address high risk emotional situations consistently with your Three Step Social Responsibility Plan and; 3) keep a running analysis of how well you are doing managing your emotions by identifying and correcting your irresponsible thinking on your Situation Response Analysis Log.

Basic Human Emotions: 101- Another high risk situation that can trigger harmful behavior is unwanted feelings. Human beings exposed to the harmful, stressful, traumatic historical events often are left with unwanted feelings that don't go away. Three basic types of unwanted feelings are anger, anxiety and depression. These emotions range in severity from mild to severe and may be begin during the stressful event or may be delayed until much later in time. Anger can range from a mild annoyance to a moderate anger to a severe rage and may be include continuous thoughts about unjust treatment and a desire for revenge. Anxiety can range from mild social discomfort to a moderate anxiety (fear) to a severe panic attack and may include continuous thoughts about something bad happening. Depression can range from a mild sadness to a moderate feeling of depression (including feeling helpless) to suicidal despair (including feeling hopeless) and may include continuous thoughts about giving up.

Identify and Correct your Irresponsible Thinking

If you have completed workbook 1, you are already familiar with the 20 types of irresponsible thinking that can trigger harmful behavior and the corrective actions to take to block that thinking (summarized in Appendix C). If you have completed workbook 1, review the top three types if irresponsible thinking that trigger your harmful behavior (i.e., in Link 4 of the Risk Factor Chain), update your work and record that thinking below along with the corrective action you need to take when you become aware of that thinking. If you have not completed workbook 1, review Appendix C and underline all of the irresponsible thinking that you have used in the past. Then look at the material you have underlined and circle the numbers of the top three types of irresponsible thinking you have used (i.e., those categories with the most material underlined).

Irresponsible Thinking Type #1 (from the list of 20 in Appendix C) _____

Characteristics of this type of thinking that I have (things you underlined)- _____

_____

Corrective Action I need to take when I notice this thinking (from the list of 20 in Appendix C)-

_____

Irresponsible Thinking Type #2 (from the list of 20 in Appendix C) _____

Characteristics of this type of thinking that I have (things you underlined)- _____

_____

Corrective Action I need to take when I notice this thinking (from the list of 20 in Appendix C)-

_____

Irresponsible Thinking Type #3 (from the list of 20 in Appendix C) _____

Characteristics of this type of thinking that I have (things you underlined)- _____

_____

Corrective Action I need to take when I notice this thinking (from the list of 20 in Appendix C)-

_____

Monitor your irresponsible thinking closely on your Situation Response Analysis log. Putting consistent effort in to identifying and changing irresponsible thinking is one of the most important things you can do to keep from falling back into your Stress-Relapse cycle of harmful behavior. The more self-awareness of your thinking that you develop and the better you get at making the corrections listed in Appendix C, the more self-control you will develop. The more self-control you develop, the more you will avoid falling back in to your Stress-Relapse cycle. Your knowledge about how to manage your harmful behavior and avoid falling back into your cycle will increase your self-efficacy (confidence) and decrease the unwanted consequences that result from harmful behavior.

Nothing Succeeds Like Success

A track record of positive coping in difficult situations will lead to the development social-emotional maturity (e.g., increased honesty, responsibility and self-efficacy or confidence). These attributes will in turn allow for better attachments to others as well as decreased life stress, which sets the occasion for resilience in a stress management cycle.

Using Negative Coping to deal with an initial harmful behavior episode such as denial of the problem or responsibility, leads you back into your Stress-Relapse Cycle. The Stress-Relapse Cycle basically involves a circular set of events beginning with: 1) Negative Coping after a harmful behavior which involves dishonesty to avoid responsibility followed by; 2) a Cover Up to avoid detection. The energy and effort involved in covering up leads to; 3) Stress Build-Up from not being loyal to what you know is right along with worrying about being caught which increases the probability of; 4) a Slip (lapse) on concern for self/others that allows the return of self-defeating habits resulting in; 5) a Fall (relapse) into irresponsible acting out through another episode of harmful behavior. The Stress-Relapse Cycle involved in maintaining harmful behavior is summarized in Figure 4. In this cycle, stress is cumulative, it adds up until the threshold of acting out is reached and a relapse occurs.

What's in it for me?

Understanding what maintains harmful behavior is extremely important if you want to avoid returning to unhealthy, harmful behavior after you have completed treatment. However, with self-help workbooks as well as group, family and individual therapy…
"You only get out of it, what you put into it" (Greg Norman and many before him) which basically means that a self-help workbook is only as good as the honesty of the person completing it. The more honest you are, the more self-knowledge you will develop. This is critically important because knowledge is power, self-knowledge is self-control power and self-control is the key to your future success.

Figure 4.
How Harmful Behavior was Maintained: The Stress-Relapse Cycle

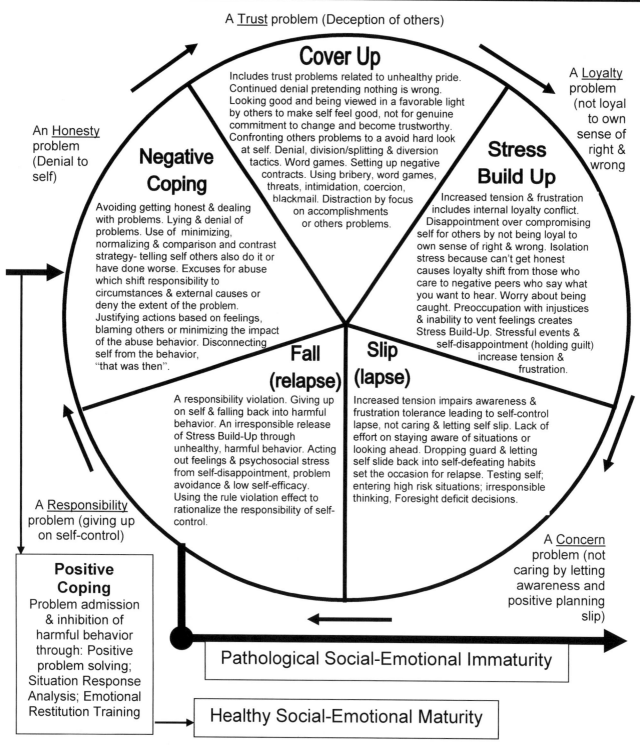

A <u>Trust</u> problem (Deception of others)

Cover Up
Includes trust problems related to unhealthy pride. Continued denial pretending nothing is wrong. Looking good and being viewed in a favorable light by others to make self feel good, not for genuine commitment to change and become trustworthy. Confronting others problems to a avoid hard look at self. Denial, division/splitting & diversion tactics. Word games. Setting up negative contracts. Using bribery, word games, threats, intimidation, coercion, blackmail. Distraction by focus on accomplishments or others problems.

A <u>Loyalty</u> problem (not loyal to own sense of right & wrong

An <u>Honesty</u> problem (Denial to self)

Negative Coping
Avoiding getting honest & dealing with problems. Lying & denial of problems. Use of minimizing, normalizing & comparison and contrast strategy- telling self others also do it or have done worse. Excuses for abuse which shift responsibility to circumstances & external causes or deny the extent of the problem. Justifying actions based on feelings, blaming others or minimizing the impact of the abuse behavior. Disconnecting self from the behavior, "that was then".

Stress Build Up
Increased tension & frustration includes internal loyalty conflict. Disappointment over compromising self for others by not being loyal to own sense of right & wrong. Isolation stress because can't get honest causes loyalty shift from those who care to negative peers who say what you want to hear. Worry about being caught. Preoccupation with injustices & inability to vent feelings creates Stress Build-Up. Stressful events & self-disappointment (holding guilt) increase tension & frustration.

Fall (relapse)
A responsibility violation. Giving up on self & falling back into harmful behavior. An irresponsible release of Stress Build-Up through unhealthy, harmful behavior. Acting out feelings & psychosocial stress from self-disappointment, problem avoidance & low self-efficacy. Using the rule violation effect to rationalize the responsibility of self-control.

Slip (lapse)
Increased tension impairs awareness & frustration tolerance leading to self-control lapse, not caring & letting self slip. Lack of effort on staying aware of situations or looking ahead. Dropping guard & letting self slide back into self-defeating habits set the occasion for relapse. Testing self; entering high risk situations; irresponsible thinking, Foresight deficit decisions.

A <u>Responsibility</u> problem (giving up on self-control)

A <u>Concern</u> problem (not caring by letting awareness and positive planning slip)

Positive Coping
Problem admission & inhibition of harmful behavior through: Positive problem solving; Situation Response Analysis; Emotional Restitution Training

Pathological Social-Emotional Immaturity

Healthy Social-Emotional Maturity

Note: Social Maturity = Honesty, trust, loyalty, concern & responsibility
Emotional Maturity = Self-awareness, self-efficacy & self-control

The Stress-Relapse Cycle: Phase 1- Negative Coping

"To thine own self be true"-- William Shakespere (1564- 1616)

Name: _____   **Date:** _____

Definition: Negative Coping can happen after a single harmful behavior episode or a period of unhealthy, harmful behavior. Negative coping involves both what you think and what you do after committing a harmful behavior. Negative coping is responsibility avoidance, not admitting that you have a problem to yourself (lying to yourself, denial), not accepting and not working on the problem by using excuses that justify your actions based on feelings triggered by others, shift the responsibility to situations and blame others, minimize/deny the extent of the problem or disconnect self from the behavior, "that was then, this is now". Negative coping is particularly damaging to honesty and continued use can wear honesty down completely. In summary, Negative coping is coping with problems in an unhealthy negative way and involves a basic honesty problem (not getting honest with yourself about having a problem, about his serious it is or about how it effects others).

Relapse Cycle Question # 1: After making a mistake and falling back into harmful behavior, what did you tell yourself to deal with it?

Three Basic Types of Negative Coping

Since there are many different ways that people try to avoid responsibility, there are an many different types of Negative Coping. Three basic types of Negative Coping are: 1) Minimizing/normalizing; 2) Justifying actions and; 3) the Victim view/blaming. Selected harmful behavior examples are provided in Table 8. In general, minimizing involves playing the behavior down and is often identified by the use of the words "just" and "only". Normalizing is making it seem like the behavior is fairly normal, often by comparing it to what others do, "It's no big deal, everyone does it." Justifying actions based on feelings involves telling yourself that

Table 8.
Three Basic Types of Negative Coping: Selected Harmful Behavior Examples
(Source: Table 2.3, p. 94 in Yokley 2008)

Harmful Behavior	Minimizing/ Normalizing	Justifying actions	Victim View/ Blaming
Trust Abuse	"I'm not lying, just avoiding"	"I didn't like their tone, so I lied to them"	I had to lie, they don't understand
Substance Abuse/ Unhealthy eating	"It was only beer, not drugs"/ "It's just one cookie"	"Anyone would get high after what happened"/ "I had to eat chocolate, I was so upset".	Relapse wasn't my fault, she left me/ "They made me overeat by taking me to my favorite restaurant"
Property Abuse	"I just stole from a store, it's insured"	"I had to take it, I needed the money to get high"	"It's not my fault that I don't have money"
Physical Abuse	"I only slapped her once"	"They made me hit them by getting me angry"	"I shouldn't be blamed, they started it"
Sexual Abuse	"I just fondled them, I didn't rape them"	"I had to do it to them, they got me worked up by flirting"	"It was their fault, they shouldn't have been flirting"

the harmful behavior was justified by the feelings that were triggered, for example "I got so upset, I had to do it". The victim view and blaming in general involves shifting the focus off of self, not taking responsibility and putting it on others. For example, "It wasn't my fault", "They started it", "They made me do it", "I couldn't help it", "They didn't give me a chance". Further description is provided in Appendix C, number 15, 16 and 18).

An important part of social maturity is honesty which depends on how aware you are of your thoughts, feelings and behaviors. Please mark how often you have been aware of using the Negative Coping methods involved in your Stress-Relapse Cycle on the following scales below.

At this point, if you did not complete Workbook 1- The Risk Factor Chain, go to Appendix F (page 132) and complete the Awareness and Honesty Exam.

A. Review your Awareness and Honesty Exam (in Appendix F, page 132 or Link#4 in Workbook 1) and record your Negative Coping ratings in the spaces provided below.

Negative Coping (16 items from Awareness and Honesty Exam, Appendix F.)

____ 15) I didn't do it that much, was upset or high	____ 56) Felt "This isn't right" after a mistake
____ 16) Told yourself it wasn't your fault or you always get blamed	____ 57) Made a mental list of why it was OK
	____ 66) Refusal to accept responsibility
____ 17) Justified actions based on feelings	____ 75) Others did it with me or got me into it
____ 35) Minimizing problem frequency or severity	____ 76) Blamed others for causing it
	____ 79) Since no one said anything, it's OK
____ 36) Blamed someone for encouraging you	____ 98) Comparing self to those with more serious problems
____ 37) Given explanations to justify mistakes	____ 99) I'm not hurting anyone but myself
____ 55) "It wasn't that wrong" or "others have done it also"	____116) Normalizing harmful behavior
	____129) Blame others for negative impact

B. Use the numbers on the rating scale below to rate how often you have had the following reactions when thinking over an episode or period of harmful behavior.

0	1	2	3	4
Never	Once	A Few Times	Often	Very Frequently

____ 1) Gone into social withdrawal (isolated yourself and avoided others) and not discussed your harmful behavior with anyone.

____ 2) Told yourself that the harmful behavior wasn't your responsibility or was due to problem circumstances (i.e., made excuses about why it wasn't your fault).

____ 3) Told yourself that the problem wasn't that serious or "If it was that serious, why didn't someone say something or take action to stop me?"

____ 4) Thought that your actions were justified based on feelings you were having (e.g., Told yourself, "I couldn't help it, I was so angry, anxious, depressed, excited, etc.").

Use the numbers on the rating scale below to rate how often you have had the following reactions when thinking over an episode or period of harmful behavior.

0 Never	1 Once	2 A Few Times	3 Often	4 Very Frequently

____ 5) Thought that others were to blame for triggering feelings which led to your behavior (e.g., Told yourself, "He/she got me started, suggested it or made me do it").

____ 6) Told yourself that the impact of the harmful behavior on others or the potential consequences to yourself were minimal (e.g., Told yourself, "I just or only did it on one occasion or could have gone further but stopped myself").

____ 7) Compared yourself with others who have done worse and thought that you aren't that bad.

____ 8) Promised yourself that you will never get in over your head with this type of problem again while telling yourself that you can handle it but this was just bad luck?

____ 9) Told yourself "that was in the past", "that was then, this is now" or "ancient history" and focused your mind on something else.

____ 10) Told yourself that you are a good person because of your positive qualities or abilities and that you don't need help because your harmful behavior was an exception rather than a rule about your behavior.

____ 11) Reassured yourself that "everything is under control" and there is no need to worry because no one will find out?

____ 12) Told yourself that there is really no problem because no consequences have occurred?

____ 13) Told someone that the trouble you were in "just happened" like an auto accident or that you "caught a case" (legal charge) like it was a cold, something you just get and rarely have anything to do with.

____ 14) Flat out lied about the behavior, denying that you ever did it.

____ 15) Made promises without really meaning it just to get people off your back.

____ 16) Felt worse about being caught (looking bad), than about what I did.

____ 17) Felt angry at yourself for getting caught, called yourself stupid and made a promise to yourself not to get caught again as opposed to telling yourself you wouldn't do it again.

____ 18) Refused to ask for help or bring things out in the open and made people aware of the problem so that they could help me.

19) What else have you thought, said or done, to cope AFTER a single episode or period of harmful behavior that was negative or didn't help you face the problem?

_____

_____

_____

_____

_____

_____

_____

Study your highest ratings in section A and B above and use the space below to record how you can use this Negative Coping knowledge in your relapse prevention plan update at the end of this section.

_____

_____

_____

_____

_____

_____

_____

C. Circle at least your top three highest Negative Coping ratings in Section A and B above. Then record those Negative Coping statements on the Stress-Relapse Cycle worksheet (page 101) at the end of this section. If some of the your choices have ratings that are ties, record the statement that applies most on the first page worksheet diagram and put the rest on the second page "continued" portion of your worksheet.

Summary Completion Instructions- Imagine yourself teaching someone else about this part of your life. Put your important descriptions in phrase form that makes it easy for you to explain and makes sense when read by others. Don't limit yourself to the top three points if there are important parts that fit in this area. Make sure that you do not leave out any important information about yourself on this topic. Use the "continued" portion if needed.

Use the space below to describe your worst period of Negative Coping.
Include how that Negative Coping led you into even more problems than if you just used positive coping and got honest. Tell what you can do about it now. Use the workspace on page 99 if needed.

_____

_____

_____

_____

Learning **Positive Coping** is a necessary first step that you need to take in order to break your harmful behavior maintenance cycle and begin to extinguish your harmful behavior by developing a stress-management cycle. Positive coping involves having the personal courage to hold yourself accountable by admitting a mistake or problem and then developing your insight and awareness while working on a solution through Situation Response Analysis. Make an added effort to focus on generating more Positive Coping responses to the problem situations you encounter each day and improve in holding yourself accountable on your Situation Response Analysis Log (Appendix D) by documenting every problem situation that you encounter.

The ART of Social Responsibility Therapy: Blocking Negative Coping [9]

Awareness training- Know the three basic types of negative coping. Get honest with yourself about what applies to you beginning with developing your awareness of minimizing, justifying and taking the victim view. Discuss your negative coping with your treatment group, care circle, sponsor or therapist.

Responsibility training- Learn to go to the opposite extreme[4] of negative coping with positive coping. Accept that in the long run you can't avoid trouble by avoiding responsibility. A summary description of going to the opposite extreme with positive coping to block negative coping is presented in Table 9.

Tolerance training- Learn to tolerate mistakes without blowing consequences out of proportion. Learn to tolerate situations by connecting thoughts and feelings after a behavior mistake. Don't disconnect self or act feelings out, learn to "sit with the sensation".

Table 9.
Going to the Opposite Extreme with Positive Coping

Negative Coping	Positive Coping
An Honesty Problem (Not getting honest with self)	(Going to the opposite extreme) Getting honest with self about mistakes/problems "To thine own self be true"
Responsibility Avoidance (avoiding dealing with problems, denial to self)	Responsibility Acceptance (accepting you made a mistake or have a problem). Use the reality scales- Will getting honest with myself about my problem stop my heart and breathing?
Minimizing Normalizing	Use role reversal, engrossment- it is a big deal, find use of "just" and "only". Others doing it, does not make it right. Use language of responsibility- "I" statements, "I did...", not "it just happened".
Justifying actions based on feelings (venting on others)	Justify actions based on facts. Find the facts. Don't compare what you did to what others have done, compare it to what's right. Think it through with the reality scales.
The victim view/blaming	"If you blame other people for your behavior, you give them control over your life". Talk about self not others, next word after "but" is..

Breaking the Relapse Cycle

"You are only limited by your creativity"[4] in coming up with ways to go to the opposite extreme to block negative coping and break the relapse cycle. Any ACTS skill (see pages 17- 27) that addresses negative coping should be applied. "Think it through" is an ACTS skill that is very useful in addressing negative coping.

"Think it Through" with the Reality Scales

Use the Reality Scales (rated on a 0- 10 scale) to "think though" the need to use negative coping and to help you break your cycle by getting honest with yourself. Start by listing your most recent fall into harmful behavior. What was it? (e.g., harmful eating, drinking, drugging, slugging, spending, sex, etc.). _____.

Then rate the need to use negative coping to deal with it on the scales below...

1. Survival Scale- "How necessary for my survival is it for me to use negative coping by minimizing my harmful behavior, justifying it or telling myself it wasn't my fault?"
   0 = not necessary; 10 = necessary to save my life _____

2. Success Scale- "How important is it to my success in life for me to use negative coping by minimizing my harmful behavior, justifying it or telling myself it wasn't my fault?"
   0= not important at all; 10= so important I will never succeed in life without it _____

3. Severity Scale- "How severe could the consequences be if I get honest with myself about my harmful behavior? (Remember, getting honest with yourself does not mean telling others)
   0= not severe at all; 10= so severe I can't stand it and will need help to let it go _____

Looking over the scale ratings above, do you really have to use negative coping to survive or succeed in life? ___Yes; ___No. Are the consequences of letting negative coping go to too severe for you to handle? ___Yes; ___No. What do you need to do about your negative coping?

_____
_____
_____
_____

Using negative coping and not getting honest with yourself about a problem puts you at risk for trying to cover it up. Discuss positive coping with your therapist or group (see Exhibit 2, p. 105).

Get honest about your Negative Coping with your therapist or treatment group. Log the date you discussed your Negative Coping and who you discussed it with in the space provided below.

Date: _____   Discussed with: _____

"Three can keep a secret if two of them are dead"-- Benjamin Franklin (1706-1790)

Name: _____   **Date:** _____

Definition: Cover-Up tactics involve trying to avoid consequences. These tactics are driven by unhealthy pride to avoid social consequences (i.e., fear of looking bad, "What will people say?") and/or fear of actual legal consequences (i.e., "What could happen to me if people find out?"). Cover-Up tactics to avoid social consequences are damage control strategies to protect image based on the attitude that it is, "It's better to look good than to admit mistakes" and "How other people view me is more important than how I really am". Cover-Up tactics to avoid legal consequences justify actions (i.e., trust abusing cover up tactics) based on feelings (i.e., fear of incarceration) and are implemented to make self feel better (i.e., less anxious) not for genuine commitment to change or to maintain real trust. However, "bargaining" by promising self, others or God, "If you just let me slide this once, I will change and never do it again", is common if the possible consequences are serious. Cover-Up involves actively attempting to block others from telling the truth about your behavior by the use of lying, misleading others, manipulation, pretending everything's normal, negative contracts, bribery, threats, coercion, intimidation or blackmail) also involves covering for others. Cover Up also involves tactics to stop people from learning the truth or even looking into it. Unhealthy Pride and misplaced priorities combine to create an image problem where how others view you becomes more important than who you really are and what you do, i.e., "It's better to look good than to do good". This image problem behavior is based on acceptance by others (usually a certain group), not on what is right, appropriate, socially beneficial or mature. This leads to an "Image over Integrity" damage control strategy involving a rush to rebuild trust, get back to looking good and being viewed in a favorable light by others to make self feel good, not as the result of a genuine commitment to change and become trustworthy,

Cover-up tactics are not limited to self but can involve covering for others as well, e.g., teens covering up peer behavior by misleading authorities, children covering-up parent neglect through dishonesty with their social workers, wives covering-up domestic violence through dishonesty with the police or company employees covering-up consumer fraud through dishonesty with investigators. While it is easy to see the self-preservation motivation of covering-up for self, covering up for others can also stem from self-preservation, not just threats or blackmail (e.g., child or spouse belief that they have to cover up because they can not survive without their significant other; employee belief that they have to cover up because if fired, they will never find another job). Covering up for others can also relate to self-blame, for example the child or spouse who tells themselves, "If I just get better grades, look better, cook better, do better, be better, they won't treat me this way". In summary, Cover-Up involves a basic trust problem (i.e., not trusting others to understand the problem or be fair with consequences, reinforced by fear of social and/or legal consequences).

Relapse Cycle Question # 2: What did you do to keep your harmful behavior from being detected or to avoid consequences?

Three basic Types of Cover Up

Threats, intimidation, coercion, blackmail and bribery are not the only methods used to keep others quiet and Cover Up problems. Since there are many different ways that people try to avoid consequences, there are an many different types of Cover Up tactics. Three basic Cover Up tactics are: 1) Deception (lying); 2) Diversion and; 3) Division. Deception which primarily involves lying includes, actively setting up negative contracts (e.g., "I'll cover for you if you cover for me") to cover up problems and prevent being caught. Deception also includes word games such as: omitting key pieces of information (i.e., dishonesty by omission); reframing the situation in a context that makes it look common/normal, socially acceptable or better and; rephrasing statements to put a positive or less negative light or "spin" on the situation. In addition, deception can involve assenting (i.e., agreeing with no intent to comply), appeasing (i.e., telling people what they want to hear), threats and bribery to deceive others by keeping things quiet. If the harmful behavior can be denied (i.e., there is no rock solid evidence) pretending nothing is wrong, acting like nothing happened and everything is normal returning to the regular everyday routine may be used to keep people from talking about the harmful behavior. If hospitalized, this is seen by a "Flight into Health" which involves pretending nothing is wrong and everything is fine. If the harmful behavior can't be denied, attempts to keep people quiet include manipulative apology (e.g., "I'm really sorry. There's no need to say anything about this, I've learned my lesson"), appeasing (e.g., "This isn't what it looks like, I can explain..."), assenting (e.g., empty promises- "I'll never do it again" with no intent to change) and negative contracts (e.g., "I'll cover for you if you cover for me").

Diversion which involves misleading others is done in several different ways involved diverting the focus away from your harmful behavior. Misleading others through impression formation tactics to cover up negative behavior involves diverting the focus to your accomplishments and good points such as good work, good grades, good community deeds. This helps cover up your problem by pretending you are doing extremely well. Diverting the focus by talking about others problems that are worse, covers up yours by taking the heat off of you and diverting the focus from your real problem to another issue (e.g., "I was drunk/high at the time") covers up your real problem. Two other diversion tactics are, "throwing out a bone" and the "diversion sandwich". "Throwing out a bone" misleads others much like what would happen if you were cooking a T-bone steak on the grill and a large dog began running strait toward you. If you ripped the bone out and tossed it, the dog would go after the bone, meanwhile you still have the meat. In this way, confessing to minor problem to avoid discussing a major one sends those confronting you after the bone while your real problem remains covered up. For example, "throwing out a bone" happens when a teenager on probation confesses to a misdemeanor by admitting that he smells like smoke because he was smoking cigarettes under age to avoid discussion of a felony (i.e., that he was actually smoking marijuana and had a cigarette afterwards to cover it up). Feeding people a "diversion sandwich" involves sandwiching a statement about your negative behavior in between two positive behavior statements to cover up the negative behavior. For example, a young man with a drug problem tells his mother, "I'm going to the library, to Jerry's (a druggie friend) and then to the church youth group". Because the library and church youth group are positive, mom assumes that Jerry must be positive.

Division is a Cover-up damage control technique involving playing people against each other also referred to as "splitting". This "divide and conquer" strategy involves abuser attempts to take the focus off of self by getting others into conflicts in order to prevent them from agreeing or arriving at a consensus about your problem. Dividing others by creating a communication breakdown so that knowledge about your behavior can't be shared is an attempt to avoid, delay or decrease consequences. Division can involve playing one authority against another or playing friends against the victim, accuser, witness or anyone confronting your harmful behavior.

Covering up is particularly damaging to trust and continued use can destroy ability to be trusted by others and trust in others.

A. Review your Awareness and Honesty Exam (in Appendix F, page 132 or Link#4 in Workbook 1) and record your Cover Up ratings in the spaces provided below.

Cover-Up (15 items from Awareness and Honesty Exam, Appendix F.)

___ 1) Told others what they wanted to hear	___101) Silence to avoid honesty
___ 11) Felt that you can't show emotions or admit mistakes	___110) Avoiding or blocking out problems
___ 31) Worry about being put down	___117) Changing the subject
___ 41) Left out parts of a story	___127) Enabling- Covering for others
___ 61) Lied or covered up to avoid consequences	___136) Played people against each other to avoid consequences
___ 63) Negative contracting- Mutual cover-up	___144) Throwing people off track by admitting a less serious problem
___ 69) Winning by intimidation	___150) Shifting responsibility to others
___ 81) Purposeful vagueness	

B. Use the numbers on the rating scale below to demonstrate your awareness of how often you have used the following Cover Up methods after a harmful behavior or episode.

0	1	2	3	4
Never	**Once**	**A Few Times**	**Often**	**Very Frequently**

___ 1) Told others that the harmful behavior wasn't your responsibility or was due to problem circumstances (i.e., gave reasons to others of why it wasn't your fault)?

___ 2) Told others that the problem wasn't that serious or "if it was that serious, why didn't someone say something or take action to stop me?"

___ 3) Told others that your actions were justified based on the feelings you had (e.g., Told others, "I couldn't help it, I was so angry, anxious, depressed, excited, etc.")?

Use the numbers on the rating scale below to demonstrate your awareness of how often you have used the following Cover Up methods after a harmful behavior or episode.

0	1	2	3	4
Never	Once	A Few Times	Often	Very Frequently

____ 4) Told others that your behavior was the fault of those who triggered the feelings which led to it (e.g., Told others, "He/she got me started, suggested it or made me do it")?

____ 5) Told others that the impact of the harmful behavior on others or the potential consequences to yourself were minimal (e.g., Told others, "I just or only did it on one occasion or could have gone further but stopped myself")?

____ 6) Set up a negative contract to prevent disclosure of the harmful behavior (i.e., Tried to get others to feel at least partially responsible so they would keep it too themselves)?

____ 7) Diverted others away from your problems by calling attention to and focusing on the accomplishments or positive things that you have done?

____ 8) Diverted others away from your problems by focusing on their problems?

____ 9) Diverted others away from your problems by focusing on other problems that required your attention such as relationship problems or family problems?

____ 10) Played people against each other or got them angry at each other to prevent them from talking to each other about you or agreeing that you have a problem.

____ 11) Tried to keep busy and active to avoid thinking too much about your problems or getting upset about them?

____ 12) Pretended everything was all right around others even if they suspected that you were troubled about something and asked you if everything was OK?

____ 13) Been purposefully nice to people who know your harmful behavior victims or are close to those who have seen your harmful behavior in order to make your harmful behavior seem unlikely or out of character if it is disclosed?

____ 14) Misleading others about your behavior by "Acting as if" everything is OK and going back to your everyday routine like nothing happened (i.e., keeping a low profile or laying low and trying not to draw attention to yourself)?

____ 15) Misleading others about your behavior by striving to look good or get recognition for doing something positive (i.e., using achievements as a cover-up diversion away from your behavior).?

____ 16) Tried hard to become liked, popular or accepted as a guard or insurance against being suspected of abusive behavior?

____ 17) Continued denying that there were any problems despite repeated questioning by others?

____ 18) Told yourself "If they don't ask the right question, I don't have to give the right answer" and denied any problems just because a minor detail was wrong despite the fact the most of it was right?

___19) Played word games to avoid giving a strait answer?

___20) Used bribery to keep others quiet?

___21) Used blackmail to keep others quiet (e.g., threatening to tell about something they did, if they tell what you did or convincing them if they talk, they will get in trouble too)?

___22) Used threats, intimidation or coercion to keep others quiet?

___23) Confessed to a minor problem (or misdemeanor) in order to avoid being confronted about a major problem (or felony), known as "Throwing out a bone" for others to chase after.

___24) Confessed to a minor problem as a manipulation to ask others to put in a good word for you and smooth over that problem as opposed to apologizing and making a commitment to change, known as a "triangulation" manipulation where you speak through others in a triangle as opposed to directly to them in a strait line.

25) What else have you said or done to help smooth over or cover up a single episode or period of harmful behavior? Discuss this with your treatment group and/or therapist. Include their feedback.

_____

_____

_____

C. Circle at least your top three most frequent Cover Up ratings in Section A and B above. Then record those Cover Up methods on the Stress-Relapse Cycle worksheet (page 101) at the end of this section. If some of the your choices have ratings that are ties, record the statement that applies most on the first page worksheet diagram and put the rest on the second page "continued" portion of your worksheet. **Summary Completion Instructions-** Imagine yourself teaching someone else about this part of your life. Put your important descriptions in phrase form that makes it easy for you to explain and makes sense when read by others. Don't limit yourself to the top three points if there are important parts that fit in this area. Make sure that you do not leave out any important information about yourself on this topic and include what you can do about it now. Use the "continued" portion if needed.

Use the space below to describe your worst Cover Up example.
Include how Covering Up your issues led you into even more problems.

_____

_____

_____

_____

_____

_____

_____

In order to counter the Cover-Up habit that you used to deal with your abuse it is important to learn competing responses that block or inhibit the Cover-Up reaction to problems. This is best done by developing an **Open-Up** style involving healthy pride (e.g., since doing the right thing often hurts, having pride in your pain) and staying humble. In addition it is important to keep your priorities strait with your problem issues "up front". Make an additional effort to open up about mistakes during the day and be sure to record this accomplishment in the Positive Coping column of your Situation Response Analysis Log (Appendix D).

The ART of Social Responsibility Therapy: Stopping a Cover Up [9]

Awareness training- Know the three basic types of cover up tactics, become aware of your cover up tactics and the effect that using those tactics has on your level of stress, your social maturity and your relationship success.

Responsibility training- Learn to go to the opposite extreme[4] of covering-up by opening up. Don't let the fear of consequences continue your cover up. Solve the problem, don't continue to cover up and avoid dealing with the problem. A summary description of going to the opposite extreme of opening up to stop covering up is presented in Table 10.

Tolerance training- Think it through with the survival scale to accept that loss of face or freedom isn't loss of life, admit mistakes, ask for help to rebuild trust.

1. "For case examples, see the ART of Social Responsibility Therapy" (Ch. 2 in Yokley, 2008)
2. A time honored therapeutic community recovery maxim circa 1973 (Nemes, Wish and Messina, 1999)

Table 10.
Going to the Opposite Extreme by Opening Up

Cover-Up A Trust Problem (Not getting honest with others)	Open Up (Go to the opposite extreme) Get honest with others "Hold yourself accountable" [1]
Unhealthy Pride, fear (damage control from fear of social or legal consequences)	Healthy Pride, courage, Realize the reason we respect honesty so much is the tremendous consequences. Admit "honesty has its price but you don't have to pay twice". Don't put your image (unhealthy pride) before your honesty.
Threats and bribes	Apology and restitution
Deception/lying	Get honest with others about problem. Think it through with the reality scales- Will admitting my problem to others stop my heart and breathing?
Diversion and Division	Don't focus on others behavior, Solve the problem- Focus on rebuilding trust through honesty. Trust gets you what you want.
1. Once you tell others, you can't keep doing it. "Three can keep a secret if two of them are dead"	

Breaking the Relapse Cycle

"You are only limited by your creativity" in coming up with ways to go to the opposite extreme[4] to block cover up and break the relapse cycle. Any ACTS skill (See pages 17- 27) that addresses cover up behavior should be applied. "Solve the problem" and "Think it through" are ACTS skills that are very useful in addressing cover up tactics.

"Solve the Problem" with SET Social Problem Solving Skills

Use the SET Social Problem Solving skills to let your Cover-up go. Start by listing a harmful behavior problem that you have struggled with, need to get rid of, avoided dealing with, keep secret, not told others about, avoided getting help for or covered up. What is it? (e.g., harmful

eating, drinking, spending, drugging, slugging, spending, sex, etc.) _____

Then use the **SET** Social Problem Solving skills listed below to deal with it.

1. **S**et your goal- Get rid of my problem (listed above) and get the life I want.
2. **E**valuate your progress and options-
   Progress (How well has what I have tried worked?): Admit that negative coping led to cover-up. List the negative coping and cover up tactics you have used- _____

   _____

   Did your negative coping solve the problem? ___Yes; ___No
   Did covering up the problem solve it? ___Yes; ___No
   Options are (What could I do at this point?):
   a) Continue negative coping and cover up to try and avoid consequences (look at your progress above, did this help? ___Yes; ___No) or;
   b) Try positive coping, get honest, open up, accept consequences and get help.
   List the consequences you would have to accept if you got honest and got help

   _____

   _____

3. **T**ake responsible action- Since dishonesty is disrespect, stop being disrespectful and get honest. Use the reality scales below to weigh out the truth about your need to cover up. The reality scales won't work for you unless you get real with yourself about three important facts: 1) "Honesty has its price but the good news is you don't have to pay twice"; 2) If others are involved, you might as well just tell because, "Three can keep a secret if two of them are dead" (Benjamin Franklin) and; 3) High numbers on the reality scales don't mean you can't stand it, they just mean you don't want to deal with it.

"Think it Through" with the Reality Scales

Use the Reality Scales (rated on a 0- 10 scale) to "think though" the need to cover up your harmful behavior and to help you break your cycle by getting honest with others. Start by copying the harmful behavior problem you have struggled with that you listed in the "Solve the Problem" section here your most recent fall into harmful behavior. What was it? (e.g., harmful

eating, drinking, spending, drugging, slugging, spending, sex, etc.) _____

Then rate the need to continue to cover that problem up.

1. Survival Scale- "How necessary for my survival is it for me to cover up my harmful behavior?"
   0 = not necessary; 10 = necessary to save my life _____

2. Success Scale- "How important is it to my success in life for me to cover up my harmful behavior?"
   0= not important at all; 10= so important I will never succeed in life without it _____

3. Severity Scale- "How severe could the consequences be if I let go of my cover up and get honest with others about my harmful behavior?
   0= not severe at all; 10= so severe I can't stand it and will need help to let it go _____

Looking over the scale ratings above, do you really have to use cover ups to survive or succeed in life? ___Yes; ___No. Are the consequences of letting your cover up go and getting honest to too severe for you to handle? ___Yes; ___No. If you believe that continuing to cover up is not necessary for survival or success and you can stand the consequences but you just don't want them, then what do you need to do about your cover up?

_____

_____

Being your brother's keeper: In group, blend your Confrontation with Concern
Sometimes people who are not getting real with themselves will frustrate you because you have been there and know what the real deal is. When this happens, it is a social responsibility for those who are doing better to help those who are struggling. This is Step 12 of Twelve Step programs. In Therapeutic Community programs, "You are your brother's keeper" or "Each one teach one" is your social responsibility. Since many with harmful behavior have been hurt as well (e.g., Fehrenbach et al., 1986) it is important to blend your confrontation of harmful behavior with concern for the person's welfare.
"If your only tool is a hammer, all of your clients will look like nails" (Fritz Perls).
"If your only tool is glue, all of your clients will look like they can bond".
Begin your confrontation of Cover-up behavior with concern, "I'm really worried that if you don't open up about what's going on with you, it's going to blow up into severe consequences. You need to get honest now."

The Consequences of Deception, Diversion and Division
Maintaining Cover Up tactics requires a great deal of mental concentration and emotional energy Cover up requires remembering what was said to who, when it was said it and why. The more you lie the more you have to remember. When you stop relying on truth you have to rely on memory. Other consequences of cover up are having to redirect emotions by generating anger at others for minor injustices in order to keep from being overwhelmed with anxiety about being uncovered or guilt about their own wrongdoing. Not trusting others enough to get honest about your problem and continuing to cover it up, increases stress build up. Keeping up this energy draining front, eventually is too much and the Stress Build Up results in a slip.

Get honest about your Cover Up methods with your therapist or treatment group. Log the date you discussed your Cover Up methods and need to Open up (see Exhibit 2, p. 105) below.

Date: _____   Discussed with: _____

"The truth shall set you free"-- John 8:32

Name: _____   Date: _____

Definition: Stress Buildup results from Cover Up because refusal to accept responsibility, lack of effort on solving the problem and not opening up to deal with feelings all increase stress. Worrying about being caught or the discovery cover up tactics that you used to prevent detection of your behavior is a common source of Stress Build-Up. Cover up dishonesty increases stress because you have to always be on your guard and remember your cover stories to avoid detection. Shifting loyalty from responsible people who tell you what you need to hear to irresponsible people who tell you what you want to hear, relieves the stress of being confronted with the truth but isolates you from people who care enough to help. Stress Buildup includes increased tension and frustration from self-disappointment over compromising yourself for others, going along to get along and not being loyal to your own sense of right and wrong and going against your better judgment. Another source of Stress Build-Up is isolation and alienation due to not being able to get close to anyone because you can't get honest with them about problems. This sets the occasion for shifting loyalty from family and true friends who care about you and say what you need to hear to negative peers who don't really know you and just say what you want to hear. Stress buildup indicators include cold, sweaty hands, headache, muscle tension, social withdrawal, short temper, nervousness, nail biting and other repetitive behaviors. In summary, Stress Buildup from not accepting responsibility for the problem, not working on it and not dealing with feelings is made worse by self-disappointment, secret keeping and holding guilt.

Relapse Cycle Question # 3: What stressful thoughts feelings and situations are you experiencing?

Three basic Contributors to Stress Build Up

Three basic contributors to Stress Build Up are: 1) Refusal to Accept Responsibility; 2) Lack of Effort and; 3) Not Dealing with Feelings. Refusal to Accept Responsibility and maintaining Cover Up tactics requires a great deal of mental concentration and emotional energy. In order to maintain a cover up, you have to remember what whey said to who, when they said it and why. This creates "lookout fatigue". The more you lie the more you have to remember. When you stop relying on truth, you have to rely on your memory. In addition, refusal to accept responsibility means isolation or loyalty shift from positive people who will confront your behavior to negative people who won't. Keeping up this energy draining front, eventually is too much and the mental Stress Build Up eventually results in a behavior slip.

Focusing all of your effort on covering up problems, means a total lack of effort on solving your problems. Lack of effort on recovery problem solving sets the occasion for rumination and self-disappointment over mistakes which further contributes to Stress Buildup. Shifting the focus from the present and your behavior to the past and other people's behavior to relieve stress builds it up further. Staying angry at others for minor issues, resentments and past injustices can distract you from feeling anxious about being caught. Unfortunately, since "the only two things you can't control in life are the past and other people's behavior", this is focusing on what you can't control which makes you feel helpless, increases depression and builds stress up.

Not opening up and dealing with feelings results in stuffing your anxiety, anger and depression. Trying not to worry about being caught including social rejection and legal consequences builds stress up. Stuffing feelings of anger at self over getting in trouble in the first place along with self-disappointment over relapse or compromising self to be accepted increases stress. Holding on to depression, feeling like a failure and guilt about caving into the harmful behavior adds further stress. In addition, stress can build up from isolation and alienation from secret keeping. You can't get close to anyone because if you can't get honest with anyone about your problem. This sets the occasion for shifting loyalty from family and true friends (positive loyalty) who care to negative acquaintances who don't really know you and say what you want to hear. Shifting loyalty to negative peers reinforces denial to self and dishonesty to others which keeps you stuck in Stress Buildup. Stuffing feelings as opposed to sharing them and discussing problems that are creating those feelings increases Stress Buildup which decreases ability to control feelings and sets the occasion for slipping up.

A. Review your Awareness and Honesty Exam (in Appendix F, page 132 or Link#4 in Workbook 1) and record your Stress Build-Up ratings in the spaces provided below.

Stress Build-Up (12 items from Awareness and Honesty Exam, Appendix F.)

____ 3) Held on to a one-sided relationship	____ 40) Hard on self about mistakes
____ 4) Told yourself its every man for himself	____ 60) Preoccupation with consequence injustices
____ 18) Thought if others aren't with me, they're against me	____ 78) Feeling I must be the best at something
____ 20) Viewed things as worse than reality	____ 82) Not asked for help
____ 21) Assenting, agreeing but not meaning it	____ 104) Ruminating- going over & over things
____ 23) Putting negative peers before positive people/family	____ 124) Denied being afraid when you were

B. Demonstrate your awareness of how often you have experienced various types of Stress Build-Up involved in your Stress-Relapse Cycle using the numbers on the rating scale below.

0	1	2	3	4
Never	Once	A Few Times	Often	Very Frequently

____ 1) Experienced a buildup of tension, frustration and stress from problems with others or things that happened to you?

____ 2) Experienced feelings of inadequacy (feeling less than others), insecurity (unsure of self) or a lack of confidence relating to problems with others or things that happened to you?

Use the numbers on the rating scale below to demonstrate your awareness of how often you have experienced various types of Stress Build-Up involved in your Stress-Relapse Cycle.

0	1	2	3	4
Never	Once	A Few Times	Often	Very Frequently

____ 3) Avoided or put off dealing with problems?

____ 4) Had problems being aware of or identifying the feelings you are having?

____ 5) Had problems controlling your feelings (i.e., found yourself leaking them out in public or in front of others by storming around or looking really upset)?

____ 6) Had problems stuffing your feelings (i.e., found yourself holding them inside and not talking to yourself in a healthy, rational, positive way about the situation involved)?

____ 7) Had problems venting your feelings in the right way (e.g., such as not asserting yourself with the person you have feelings for)?

____ 8) Compromised your values to be accepted by others or put yourself in a situation with negative others during a period of stress?

____ 9) Tried hard to do something good, achieve a good reputation, successful status or impress others to make up for feeling bad about yourself and your past behavior.

____ 10) Felt isolated from others because of not being able to get honest about problems.

____ 11) Shifted to hanging with negative peers after doing the wrong thing and away from positive peers or family to avoid feeling phony, uneasy or to avoid possible detection.

____ 12) Had Stress Build-Up over worry about getting caught.

____ 13) Dealt with own mistakes by looking at others and got caught up in injustices done by others.

____ 14) Had Stress Build-Up over worry about fitting in socially.

____ 15) Felt guilty or bad about what I did and got stressed dwelling on it.

____ 16) Had Stress Build-Up over worry about relationships.

____ 17) Wanted to talk but had tension (Stress Build-Up) because I couldn't get my feelings out.

____ 18) Had tension (Stress Build-Up) from holding guilt and knowing I was in the wrong.

____ 19) Felt guilty or bad because I was thinking about doing the harmful behavior again.

____ 20) Increased stress by putting off getting things done.

____ 21) Felt angry at myself for what I did, called myself stupid and got worked up about it.

____ 22) Increased stress by not writing things down and having conflicts over not getting things done.

Use the numbers on the rating scale below to demonstrate your awareness of how often you have experienced various types of Stress Build-Up involved in your Stress-Relapse Cycle.

0	1	2	3	4
Never	Once	A Few Times	Often	Very Frequently

____23) Felt embarrassed and ashamed about what I did and got stressed dwelling on it.

____24) Refused to talk to people about being upset and what was going on with me.

____25) Felt disgusted with myself about what I did and got stressed dwelling on it.

____26) Increased stress by not planning ahead and being caught off guard.

27) What else have you done or failed to do which caused stress to build up on you? Discuss this with your treatment group and/or therapist. Include their feedback.

_____

_____

_____

_____

_____

_____

C. Circle at least your top three highest Stress Build-Up ratings in Section A and B above. Then record those Stress Build-Up reactions on the Stress-Relapse Cycle worksheet (page 101) at the end of this section.

If some of the your choices have ratings that are ties, record the statement that applies most on the first page worksheet diagram and put the rest on the second page "continued" portion of your worksheet.

Summary Completion Instructions
Imagine yourself teaching someone else about this part of your life. Put your important descriptions in phrase form that makes it easy for you to explain and makes sense when read by others. Don't limit yourself to the top three points if there are important parts that fit in this area. Make sure that you do not leave out any important information about yourself on this topic. Use the "continued" portion if needed.

Use the space on the following page to describe the most stressful situation (or period) of your life.

Include how you carried that stress with you (i.e., the thoughts and feelings you are left with) and how you it affects your present life if you allow yourself to dwell on it. What mistakes have you made when stressed-out thinking about it? What can you do to keep stress from building up?

_____

_____

_____

_____

_____

_____

_____

_____

_____

_____

_____

_____

Developing useful **Stress-Management** methods to decrease tension and frustration are needed to block Stress Build-Up and avoid slipping into relapse. Ask for help in this area if you need it.

The ART of Social Responsibility Therapy: Relieving Stress Buildup [9]

Awareness training- Learn to identify the source of your stress buildup (e.g., unwanted feelings from poor decisions, excuses not to try, working yourself up over things you can't change) and the irresponsible thinking that maintains it (e.g., just, only, but, should, must). Remember "JOBS are a Must" is a good memory trick to help you recognize irresponsible thinking. The words "just" and "only" help you recognize when you are "minimizing" stress, playing it down, trying to ignore it (e.g., "I just started to..." or "I only did it a little"). The word "but" helps your recognize excuses, not taking responsibility (e.g., "Yes, but it wasn't my fault"), the "I can't belief" ("Why even try, I can't do it") or justifying (e.g., "I deserved a reward for doing good" or "They deserved what they got for working me up"). The words "should" and "must" helps patients recognize that they are being irrational (e.g., "Friends should always agree with me") or unrealistic (e.g., "I must always succeed the first time I try").

Responsibility training- Learn to go to the opposite extreme[4] of allowing stress buildup with stress adaptation skills. Stop stuffing feelings and use responsible assertiveness to vent feelings to the right people at the right time. Get real with yourself about, "What's in it for me to get honest?" and admit that secret keeping avoids solving problems which builds up stress while getting honest with yourself and getting help solves problems which relieves stress. Admit that, "The truth shall set you free" (John 8:32) from stress. Stress doesn't cause you to act out feelings through harmful behavior, stress build up without a positive release valve does. Find a positive outlet for your feelings. Learn to walk it off and talk it off with a responsible friend (i.e., who has solid honesty, trust, loyalty, concern and responsibility), sponsor or therapist who will tell you what you need to hear not what you want to hear. A summary description of going to the opposite extreme with stress adaptation to relieve stress buildup is presented in Table 11.

Remember, compromising yourself for others putting them first all the time creates stress buildup but telling yourself "You've got to look out for number one" can make you selfish You need to achieve a balance by reminding yourself, "You're number one but there are other numbers." In order to prevent stress buildup and put a HALT to relapse, you need to take care of yourself by not getting too Hungry, Angry, Lonely or Tired. When you are isolated, loneliness and boredom are likely and getting needs for attention, acceptance or excitement met through positive social interactions is unlikely. This sets you up for justifying relapse actions based on loneliness feelings. Realize that moods change but the consequences of justifying actions based on feelings don't change. Shift your thinking from the negative things about you to the opposite extreme positive things you value. Focus on your honesty, trust, loyalty, concern and responsibility as competing factors to harmful behavior. Think about it, you can't be dishonest and irresponsible while being honest about your cravings and responsible by opening up about your slips with your treatment group, care circle, sponsor or therapist.

Tolerance training- Learn to rebuild loyalty to positive significant others and what you know is right is right. Work on an apology for your harmful behavior that takes responsibility for your behavior and clarifies how you got your problem along with what kept it going and what you have learned to interrupt it. If the harmful behavior has been serious (e.g., against the law) or has inflicted serious harm to others, work on your apology with a mental health professional who has experience in apology/clarification sessions and only apologize in a therapy session, never alone with the person you hurt. Use your healthy behavior success skills to tolerate stress, tolerate behavior feedback and tolerate the consequences of getting honest.
1. "For case examples, see the ART of Social Responsibility Therapy" (Ch. 2 in Yokley, 2008)
2. A time honored therapeutic community recovery maxim circa 1973 (Nemes, Wish and Messina, 1999)

Table 11.
Going to the Opposite Extreme with Stress Adaptation

Stress Buildup- A Loyalty problem Results from not being loyal to what you know is right (own sense of right and wrong) and who you know is right (positive people), taking on too much	**Stress Adaptation** (Go to the opposite extreme be loyal to who you know is right and what you know is right) "Do the right thing"
Increased Tension	Cope with Tension
Isolation from secret keeping, stuffing feelings and not discussing problems, refusal to accept responsibility for actions and self (taking on too much, doing for others avoids dealing with self)	**Think it through** with the reality scales to help you discuss feelings and problems. Use the mirror concept (p. 86)- Get feedback from positive people to better see your behavior.
Anxiety about cover-up tactics not working, being caught, consequences from lack of effort to solve the problem	Stop avoiding the problem and **Solve the problem**, Use social problem solving skills
Not dealing with feelings such as self-disappointment or anger over caving into behavior urges	Use your mistakes to make a relapse prevention plan, accept that honesty relieves stress and **Calm down** with the ABC's of letting feelings go

Breaking the Relapse Cycle

"You are only limited by your creativity" in coming up with ways to go to the opposite extreme[4] in order to relieve stress buildup and break the relapse cycle. Any ACTS skill (See pages 17- 27) that relieves stress buildup should be applied. "Calm down", "Think it through" and "Solve the problem" are ACTS skills that are very useful in relieving stress buildup.

The ABC's of Letting Feelings Go

Use the ABC's of Letting Feelings Go to relieve Stress Buildup and to help you break your cycle. "A" is the **A**ction that occurred (the problem situation or event); "B" is the **B**elief problem, about the action that works you up and triggers problem feelings or urges (i.e., often contains the word "should" or "must"); "C" is **C**hallenging the belief problem about the action to relieve the unwanted stressful feeling in order to stop following the feeling and let it go (i.e., to avoid justifying relapse based on stress, p. 124). Stress buildup comes with feelings that get kicked up by the actions of others and feelings we have about our own actions. If it has to do with others, it often has to do with social maturity problems (i.e., problems with honesty, trust, loyalty, concern or responsibility). Some examples of using the ABC's of Letting Feelings Go to relieve Stress Buildup from being upset with others over social maturity problems are provided in Table 12 below.

Table 12.
Relieving stress with The ABC's of letting feelings go

Honesty Problem
Action- Lazy peer didn't do their part on a project and said we were the one who didn't get things done.
Belief- "I can't take this crap. I *should* just beat the truth out of them." (triggers anger)
Challenging the belief to relieve stress- "Who said I can't take this crap? This is disturbing, but not dangerous. Anyway this lazy ass probably won't will be believed, because they've blown things off before and I haven't." (relieves anger).

Trust Problem
Action- Gossiping friend talks behind our back about something personal.
Belief- "I can't stand being embarrassed, I *must* leave and never come back." (triggers social anxiety)
Challenging the belief to relieve stress- "Where is the evidence that I can't stand being embarrassed, I don't like it but I can stand it. Besides who says a gossip will be believed." (relieves anxiety)

Loyalty Problem
Action- Good looking flirtatious partner cheats.
Belief- "This is too much to bear. It *must* mean there's something wrong with me". (triggers depression)
Challenging the belief to relieve stress- "Why does it follow that because they cheated there's something wrong with me?" (relieves depression)

Concern Problem
Action- Mean, selfish partner puts us down to build themselves up.
Belief- "I *must* not be able to do anything right." (triggers feeling inadequate)
Challenging the belief to relieve stress- "How likely is it that I really can't do anything right just because my partner gets me feeling that way? (relieves feeling inadequate)

Responsibility Problem
Action- A peer made excuses for not paying us back so we didn't have enough money for lunch.
Belief- "This *must* mean they will never pay me back. This is not right!" (triggers anger)
Challenging the belief to relieve stress- What if the worst happens and they never do pay me back? It won't stop my heart an breathing (relieves anger)

If the stressful event has to do with us, it often has to do with not getting our needs met, not meeting goals we have set, not doing well enough, not getting what we hoped for or expecting more of ourselves. Falling back into a harmful behavior, breaking our own promises, failing a test or doing poorly on a job interview, not speaking up for ourselves all result in being upset with ourselves are just a few examples. Relieving stress over being upset with yourself is the same as stress over upset about the behavior of others. The key is listening to yourself, finding the word "should" and "must" and challenging the beliefs that those words support. People talk to themselves in different ways. When some people say "I have to..." they, mean "I must" and when some people say "I need to..." they mean I should. If you look close enough, you can find the words "should" and "must" that are supporting the belief problems you need to challenge.

Now do your own example of using the ABC's to let you feelings go and relieve stress buildup. Start by listing the most recent problem situation or event that got you upset and stressed you out. What was it? (e.g., the way someone looked at you, something someone said to you or about you, something that someone did to you, something that you wanted that fell through).

Action that occurred (the problem situation or event).

_____

_____

_____

_____

Belief problem about the action that triggers unwanted feelings and builds stress up (i.e., often contains the word "should" or "must")

_____

_____

_____

_____

Challenging the words "should" or "must" that support the belief problem to relieve stress buildup by letting feelings go.

_____

_____

_____

_____

Now use the reality scales to weigh out the truth that you can stand the consequences of getting honest and letting stress buildup go, you just don't want those consequences.

"Think it Through" with the Reality Scales

Copy the Belief Problem that led to your Stress Buildup (from the ABC's of Letting Feelings Go above) to the space provided below. For example, "I can't stand it if people find out. I *must* cover this up to avoid what people will think of me or getting in trouble" (triggers stress buildup from social anxiety or fear of consequences).

_____

_____

_____

Then rate the need to continue letting stress build up (e.g., worrying about being found out or getting consequences) by not letting feelings go, continuing to cover up problems (e.g., to avoid what people will think or avoid getting consequences) and avoid working on the solution.

1. Survival Scale- "How necessary for my survival is it for me to keep letting stress build up by not letting feelings go, continuing to cover up problems and avoiding working on the solution?"
   0 = not necessary; 10 = necessary to save my life _____

2. Success Scale- "How important is it to my success in life for me to keep letting stress build up by not letting feelings go, continuing to cover up problems and avoiding working on the solution?"
   0= not important at all; 10= so important I will never succeed in life without it _____

3. Severity Scale- "How severe could the consequences be if I stop letting stress build, start letting feelings go, open up about my problems and start working on the solution?"
   0= not severe at all; 10= so severe I can't stand it and will need help to handle it _____

Looking over the scale ratings above, do you really have to keep letting stress build up by not letting feelings go, continuing to cover up problems and avoiding working on the solution?

____Yes; ____No.

Are the consequences of letting go of your stress build up, getting honest and getting help too severe for you to handle?

____Yes; ____No.

If you believe that continuing to let stress build up by not letting feelings go, continuing to cover up problems and avoiding working on the solution is not necessary for survival or success and you can stand the consequences but you just don't want them, then it's time to "solve the problem".

"Solve the Problem" with SET Social Problem Solving Skills

Use your **SET** Social Problem Solving skills to "Solve the Problem" and let Stress Buildup go.

1. **S**et your goal- For example, "Get rid of my stress, let my feelings go and feel better by opening up and getting help for my problem with (list _____).

2. **E**valuate your progress and options.

> **Progress** (How well has what I have tried worked?): Has holding onto feelings and cover-up has caused too much stress buildup? ___Yes; ___No. List other things in your life that are causing stress buildup _____
>
> _____
>
> **Options are** (What could I do at this point?):
> a) Continue to feel stress over not being loyal to what you know is right or who you know is right. Continue to avoid dealing with own feelings by focusing on others or;
> b) Relieve the stress build up by opening up, getting help, putting effort into solving the problem and dealing with your feelings. List other options _____
>
> _____

3. **T**ake responsible action- Take responsibility, open up and "get it off your chest" to relieve stress. Admit that getting help will keep you from giving up on self-control and falling back into harmful behavior again. List the harmful behavior or mistake that you need open up about in order to relieve stress and avoid relapse _____

   _____

   Name of someone who can help you that you will open up to _____

What if I don't take responsible action?
Stress buildup from not working on your problem (i.e., not getting honest with yourself about a problem and not trusting others enough to get honest with them), shifts your loyalty from those who care enough to confront you to those who don't and tell you what you want to hear. This shifting loyalty increases your stress and puts you at risk for slipping up.

Get honest about your Stress Build-Up with your therapist or treatment group. Discuss Stress Adaptation with your therapist or group (see Exhibit 2, p. 105). Log the date you discussed your Stress Build-Up and Stress Adaptation along with who you discussed it with in the space provided below.

Date: _____ Discussed with: _____

"An error doesn't become a mistake until you refuse to correct it."-- Orlando A. Battista

Name: _____   **Date:** _____

Definition: A slip (or lapse) sets the occasion for relapse. A slip occurs when we set ourselves up for failure by letting awareness, judgment or self-control go and sliding back into old negative habits. For example, dwelling on trigger thoughts or feelings, entering high risk situations or creating conflicts by leaking feelings on others. Slips are harmful behavior antecedents (i.e., things that come just before a fall and set you up to fall back into your harmful behavior) or triggers (i.e., things that start you falling back into your harmful behavior). Slips are self-defeating thoughts or behaviors set the occasion for giving up on self, letting go of self-control, and acting out feelings through harmful behavior. A slip is typically a lapse (slight error) in awareness, judgment or self-control that sets you up for falling back into unhealthy, harmful behavior, often by entering a high risk situation for relapse or not leaving a high risk situation that occurs. Although entering a high risk situation, ruminating on high risk thoughts or starting a high risk behavior are common slips, a slip can also involve letting self slide back into any type of negative self-defeating habit (e.g., score keeping and getting even). Typical examples include:
1. "Don't care" exposure to high risk situations or refusal to avoid them (judgment lapse);
2. Testing self by exposure to high risk situations (judgment lapse);
3. Careless or thoughtless exposure to high risk situations (awareness or effort lapse);
4. Not challenging irresponsible thinking or irrational beliefs (awareness or effort lapse);
5. Not challenging affect impaired attributions or perceptions which involves letting feelings influence what meaning you attribute to the behavior of others. Examples include feeling attracted towards someone and attributing their smile as meaning "they want me", feeling angry at someone and attributing their look as "they want to fight" or feeling
6. anxious around someone and attributing their comments as criticism or rejection (awareness or effort lapse);
7. Spacing out and letting awareness of the environment go (awareness lapse);
8. Making foresight deficit decisions that lead you into high risk situations (an awareness lapse);
9. Allowing yourself the luxury of Low Frustration Tolerance outbursts (self-control lapse);
10. Feeding the PIG- allowing Problem of Immediate Gratification fits (self-control lapse).

In summary, a Slip involves a basic concern problem (not caring enough about self to keep your problem a priority and letting relapse prevention planning slip usually as a result of Stress Buildup) "If you fail to plan, you plan to fail".

The definition of a slip (or lapse) has to be stricter with behavior that is harmful to others than behavior that is harmful to self. For example, the traditional substance abuse or overeaters definition, where a slip (lapse) is when you take a drink or eat a candy bar and a fall (relapse) is when you continue on a drinking or eating binge cannot be applied to physical or sexual abuse. Wife beaters and child molesters cannot be allowed to state that they only had a slip and didn't relapse because they didn't continue beating or molesting their victim after the initial assault.

With behavior that is harmful to others, the bar has to be set higher with the commission of any harmful behavior against others being considered a relapse and putting yourself in a high risk situation that could lead to relapse being considered a slip (or lapse).

Relapse Cycle Question # 4: What slips have you noticed that can lead you to fall back into your harmful behavior?

Three basic Types of Slips

There are an many different types of Slips that that set us up for falling back into our past harmful behavior. Three basic types are Slips in awareness, judgment and self-control. Examples of awareness slips include not noticing trigger thoughts, trigger feelings or trigger situations and making foresight deficit decisions. Foresight is the ability to look ahead and notice what is likely to come next. A Foresight Deficit Decision is a foresight slip that involves entering high risk situations accidently. Foresight Deficit Decisions often involve letting your positive planning slip, dropping your guard, not looking ahead, not staying aware of behavior patterns and not noticing trigger thoughts, feelings or situations. This is often the result of HALT fatigue (i.e., letting yourself get to hungry, angry, lonely or tired) which results in entering a high risk situation for falling back into harmful behavior. The bottom line is that Foresight Deficit Decisions are planning problems and with harmful behavior, "If you fail to plan, you plan to fail". Foresight deficit decisions which involve problems looking ahead to what could happen can relate to getting side tracked by good intentions. For example, a foresight deficit decision by a recovering alcoholic would be deciding to keep an unopened bottle of Jack Daniels they found under the couch while cleaning house, "just in case company comes". Please read other foresight deficit decision examples in Appendix B. Foresight deficit decisions can also relate to judgment problems.

Judgment slips are related to self-efficacy which is basically the confidence that you can be effective, do things and handle situations. Good judgment is based on a healthy sense of self-efficacy. For example, the belief that, "I can complete treatment, learn to handle my high risk situations and manage my harmful behavior if I keep trying and don't quit". Poor judgment decisions can come from grandiosity which is basically an over-confidence slip from way too much self-efficacy. For example, the belief that, "I don't need to treatment, I can handle my problem on my own without any help from so called professionals who never had this problems and don't know as much as I do about it." Other examples include putting yourself at risk for relapse by entering high risk situations on purpose due to a "No problem, I can handle it" attitude, an belief that "I should be able to handle it" and testing self to see if you can or thinking "I have to handle it, no one else can". Poor judgment decisions can also come from an "I can't" belief which is basically not enough self-efficacy. For example, the belief that, "I can't complete treatment and even if I do, I won't be able to handle the temptations of high risk situations no matter how much I try"

Self-Control Slips include slipping into a "Don't care attitude", leaking feelings and compromising yourself. Getting careless, letting refusal skills slip and going along with something wrong just to get along. Slipping into a "Don't care attitude" is a basic concern problem towards self and others, involving excuses to get lax about taking care of your self-control recovery by avoiding high risk people, places and things. Examples include telling yourself, "So what?", "I'm only hurting myself", "Who cares", "It's too hard", "Other people don't have to avoid…" (pity party). The "Don't care attitude" blocks role-reversal (i.e., putting yourself in other peoples shoes) and using fantasy fast forward (i.e., thinking the situation through to the end) which prevents considering consequences to self and others. Self-control slips that involve feelings leaking feelings out on others include aggressive, suggestive or harmful comments, verbal power struggles, having the last word and improper actions such as aggressive body language, invasion of personal space or borrowing without asking. Compromising yourself is a social pressure assertiveness slip that often involves compromising yourself to be accepted by others going along with them and doing things you know you shouldn't. For example, a recovering alcoholic accepts invitation from friends to watch the baseball playoffs on the wide screen TV at a local bar.

A. Review your Awareness and Honesty Exam (in Appendix F, page 132 or Link#4 in Workbook 1) and record your Slip/Lapse ratings in the spaces provided below.

Slip/Lapse (21 items from Awareness and Honesty Exam, Appendix F.)

___ 12) Compromising self to be accepted	___ 90) Arguing for control or fun
___ 13) Didn't write things down or get them done	___ 93) Putting things off until the last minute
___ 14) Borrowed without asking, forgetting to return	___ 94) Creating chaos, stirring up conflict
___ 19) Jumped to conclusions based on the situation	___ 111) Late and/or missed appointments
___ 39) Assuming- Made decisions without checking facts	___ 112) Relationship approach-avoidance
___ 43) Defending negative relationships	___ 113) Angry at criticism & criticized back
___ 53) Not thinking about consequences	___ 123) Not asking to avoid hearing "no"
___ 73) Failure to plan for future	___ 133) Putting others down to build self up
___ 74) Relationship jealousy or possessiveness	___ 134) Told self it's better to play others than be played
___ 88) Using emotions to get my way	___ 156) Told self it's only wrong if you get caught
	___ 160) Told self if they don't say anything, they must not care

B. Use the numbers on the rating scale below to demonstrate how aware you are of the Slips (or lapses) that were involved in your Stress-Relapse Cycle.

0	1	2	3	4
Never	**Once**	**A Few Times**	**Often**	**Very Frequently**

____ 1) Tested yourself by exposing yourself to people, places or things which were definitely high risk for triggering a relapse)?
List any personal example you can recall (Use the workspace on page 99 if needed)

_____

_____

_____

____ 2) Violated minor or unwritten, personal rules and pushed it a little further or did it again if no consequences occurred? (sometimes called "testing the limits" or "pushing back the line" on rules)
List any personal example you can recall (Use the workspace on page 99 if needed)

_____

_____

____ 3) Allowed yourself to dwell on something that you know you shouldn't be thinking about doing to the point that a plan of how or when to do it begins to take shape?
List any personal example you can recall (Use the workspace on page 99 if needed)

_____

_____

____ 4) Been told or believed that you have a problem with missing important things to look out for (i.e., not being aware of relapse triggers), dropped your guard, got lax or had a problem planning ahead to avoid trouble?
List any personal example you can recall (Use the workspace on page 99 if needed)

_____

_____

____ 5) Found yourself irritated with people who were getting on your case for doing or saying something wrong even though you clearly had no plan or intent to hurt anyone?
List any personal example you can recall (Use the workspace on page 99 if needed)

_____

_____

Use the numbers on the rating scale below to demonstrate how aware you are of the Slips (or lapses) that were involved in your Stress-Relapse Cycle.

0	1	2	3	4
Never	Once	A Few Times	Often	Very Frequently

___ 6) Allowed yourself the luxury of exhibiting Low Frustration Tolerance (LFT), Problems with Immediate Gratification (PIG) or compromising self to meet needs for acceptance, attention or excitement?

PIG problems are easily recognized by the "King Baby" fits that occur when frustrated because needs are not being immediately gratified. "Feeding the PIG" is when you let yourself fly off the handle when you don't get what you want. LFT problems involve showing no patience, having "a short fuse" and refusing to accept the responsibility of dealing with frustrations by positive problem solving or other socially mature methods that might delay getting feelings off.

List any personal example you can recall (Use the workspace on page 99 if needed)

_____

_____

___ 7) Created a crisis or stirred things up on purpose?

Since individuals with unhealthy, harmful behavior are used to crisis situations, creating a crisis in a relationship may act to level the playing field for them. Another gain is that the crisis is a temporary distraction from the abuser's behavior problem. The third hidden benefit of creating a crisis is that it provides an excuse to relapse.

List any personal example you can recall (Use the workspace on page 99 if needed)

_____

_____

___ 8) Let self slip into irresponsible thinking, making excuses, justifying or minimizing being around people, places or things that could trigger relapse?

List any personal example you can recall (Use the workspace on page 99 if needed)

_____

_____

_____

___ 9) Created a self-fulfilling prophesy (see explanation below)?

A self-fulfilling prophesy is a situation that you predict or worry will happen but cause to come true even though you, on the surface, don't want it to come true. For example, being afraid of rejection, telling yourself that the person you ask out won't say yes, then making that happen by saying, "You don't want to go out tonight do you?"

A trust abuser example would be someone who was so worried that his girlfriend would leave him for another guy that he continuously lied to her to build himself up in her eyes. In time she found out that he wasn't what he pretended to be and ended up leaving him as he predicted.

List any personal example you can recall (Use the workspace on page 99 if needed)

_____

_____

_____

Use the numbers on the rating scale below to demonstrate how aware you are of the Slips (or lapses) that were involved in your Stress-Relapse Cycle.

0	1	2	3	4
Never	**Once**	**A Few Times**	**Often**	**Very Frequently**

____10) Exposed yourself to negative social influence? How often have you associated with people (peers, partners or parents) who are a bad influence or have the same type of problems that you have and are not trying to change?

List any personal example you can recall (Use the workspace on page 99 if needed)

_____

_____

_____

____11) Made foresight deficit decisions? Foresight deficit decisions are decisions which lack foresight or the ability to look ahead and think about what could happen in various situations. This often results in thoughtless decisions to enter high risk situations leading to relapse.

Review ALL of the examples of foresight deficit decisions listed in Appendix B before rating this question and writing your own example.

Write your own example of a foresight deficit decision that you made which allowed you to slip into a harmful behavior (Use the workspace on page 99 if needed)

_____

_____

_____

_____

_____

12) What else have you thought, said or done, BEFORE a single episode or period of harmful behavior that you consider a slip that helped trigger the harmful behavior?

_____

_____

_____

C. Circle at least your top three highest ratings of Slips in Section A and B above. Then record those Slips on the Stress-Relapse Cycle worksheet (page 101) at the end of this section. If some of the your choices have ratings that are ties, record the statement that applies most on the first page worksheet diagram and put the rest on the second page "continued" portion of your worksheet.

Summary Completion Instructions- Imagine yourself teaching someone else about this part of your life. Put your important descriptions in phrase form that makes it easy for you to explain and makes sense when read by others. Don't limit yourself to the top three points if there are important parts that fit in this area. Make sure that you do not leave out any important information about yourself on this topic. Use the "continued" portion if needed.

Use the space below to describe the biggest slip that you ever made and how that led you into trouble with yourself, others, the authorities or in a relationship. Include who it involved, what the slip was, when it occurred, where it was and why you believe you made the slip (i.e., what was your motivation, want, need, goal or drive). What can you do to avoid the type of slips you have made?

_____

_____

_____

_____

_____

_____

_____

_____

_____

_____

_____

_____

_____

A **Step** is an advance in self-control or self-awareness that permits avoidance or escape from high risk or trigger situations. In order to substitute a Step for a Slip in problem situations, it is very important to "Know where you are coming from" by developing self-awareness of your thoughts and feelings along with insight or understanding your personal behavior patterns. This is referred to as knowing where you are "coming from" with your statements and actions. Put an added effort into taking a Step during problem situations that remove yourself from risk or resolve conflicts. Be sure to log your Step accomplishments on the Positive Coping column of your Situation Response Analysis Log (Appendix D).

The ART of Social Responsibility Therapy: Correcting a Slip [9]

Awareness training- become aware of High Risk Situations for relapse, foresight deficit decisions. Get honest with yourself and admit that we only say "So what?" before the consequences. Since a "Don't care attitude" must occur before and during harmful behavior in order to continue, those with a family history of harmful behavior can use that experience to consider the consequences to self and others in order to avoid a Fall.

Responsibility training- learn to go to the opposite extreme [4] of a harmful behavior slip with a step up in harmful behavior awareness, judgment and self-control. showing concern for self by leaving high risk situations, avoid trouble through positive planning and the three step Social Responsibility plan. Go to the opposite extreme from focusing on the present harmful behavior urge to focusing on the future consequences of acting on that urge. For example...

- How could an obese youth, easily eat an entire pizza while thinking about getting made fun of in gym class every day because of their weight? Or thinking about the disappointment on their mothers face if she were to see them doing this?
- How could a father of three, easily continue to drink his paycheck away while thinking about how he felt coming to school with dirty torn clothes as a child because his father drank the families money away? Or thinking about dying of liver failure like his father?
- How could a man easily continue to beat his wife while thinking about the pain of being beaten by his father when trying to stop him beating his mother? Or thinking about going to prison like his father?
- How could a youth easily continue to molest a child while thinking how humiliated and ashamed he felt when he was molested by a neighbor? Or thinking about seeing headlines of his arrest of his arrest on tomorrow mornings news paper and feeling the humiliation of public exposure, fear of long term prison or death at the hands of an enraged parent?

A summary description of going to the opposite extreme by stepping up relapse prevention efforts with stress adaptation to correct a slip is presented in Table 13.

Tolerance training- learn to tolerate high-risk emotions without leaking them on others through the ABC's of letting feelings go and the reality scales to help you "sit with the sensation" and not act on your feelings.

Table 13.
Going to the Opposite Extreme by Stepping Up Relapse Prevention

Slip (Lapse) A Concern Problem (not caring by letting awareness and relapse prevention planning slip)	Step Up (Go to the opposite extreme) by keeping your recovery a priority
Lapse in…	Tighten up on…
Awareness- Foresight slips, failure to look ahead	Awareness of high risk situations triggers use of fantasy fast forward (p. 113).
Judgment- "Pushing back the line", Entering high risk situations, "I should be able to handle it", testing self	Judgment- Hold the line. **Avoid trouble** with high risk situation avoidance and escape skills.
Self-control- Displacement of feelings (leaking), social pressure (compromising self)	Self-control- **Think it through**, avoid last word power struggles. Use concrete face saving tools.

"Acting as if" Develops Self-Control

The mask we wear in life can be more important than what we really are because over time our mask can become our identity. This is possible because, "We are what we repeatedly do"- Aristotle (384 BC-322 BC). Thus, if we know we have a harmful behavior problem with eating, drinking, drugging, slugging, spending or sex and we repeatedly stop ourselves from falling back into that behavior by "acting as if" we are different and going to the opposite extreme of that harmful behavior, eventually we become what we "act as if" we are, i.e., a healthy eating, clean and sober, self-controlled, frugal, sexually appropriate person. If I consistently "Act as if" I am the person I want to be, I am actually practicing what I want to be and in time this practice will move me towards becoming what I want to be. [2]

Knowing what you are and admitting it (e.g., "Hi, my name is James and I'm an alcoholic, drug addict, food addict, sex addict, gambling addict, shopaholic, workaholic, etc.) is considered a good first step in many treatment programs. However, knowing what you are only makes you a person with self-awareness, it does not move you towards becoming the person you want to be. Becoming the person you want to be requires that you take responsibility to practice acting like the person you want to be every day in every challenging situation. In Social Responsibility Therapy, taking responsibility for your behavior (e.g., "Hi my name is James and I am responsible for my harmful behavior) and consistently acting like the person you want to be is most important.

You don't have to be born with self-control first to become the person you want to be but you do have to act like the person they want be every day by avoiding and escaping your high risk situations for relapse if you want to develop healthy self-control habits. You don't have to actually have self-control, you just have to act as if you have it by doing the things that people with self-control do. People with self-control stay in control by not entering situations where they are likely to lose self-control and leaving situations where they are likely to lose self-control. People who don't lose self-control have learned that "Planning power beats willpower". Think about it, if I want to be sober and I start acting like a sober person, since sober don't spend all their time thinking about drinking, I need to get into some of the sober interests and activities they do. If I want to get my weight down, and I start acting like a thin person, since thin people don't spend all their time thinking about food, I need to get into some of the interests and activities they do. If I want to let go of my sexual behavior problem and I start acting like someone who is not obsessed with sex, since those people do not read pornography 24/7, I need to get into some of the non-sexual interests and activities they do. This brings us to the key word "want". You have to want to stop the harmful behavior before you will be willing to act like the people who don't have it.

If you want to learn an instrument, a language or change a behavior, you have to take the responsibility to practice what you want to sound like or be like. There's lots of motivation to practice an instrument or a sport as both will bring attention, acceptance and excitement through fame and fortune. Back to first things first. To keep from missing the point, we have to remind ourselves that celebrities want honesty, trust, loyalty, concern and responsibility. The tabloid articles about their messy break ups keep teaching us that honesty and loyalty is more important to them than image and looks. If image and looks were all it took to make a relationship work, there would be no divorce in Hollywood. Acting as if you have social maturity (i.e., honesty, trust, loyalty, concern and responsibility- remembering that our #1 responsibility is self-control) is what you need to do to get rid of what you don't want in life (i.e., unhealthy, harmful behavior habits) and get what you want in life (healthy, personal and professional relationships).

Harmful Behavior Slips: Nobody is perfect, Everybody makes mistakes

Good people have good values but they are not perfect. Values are the goals we shoot for in terms of how we want to be. How good we are at making those goals, sticking to our values being who we want to be and "doing the right thing" is a different matter. In Social Responsibility Therapy, doing the right thing is sticking to our healthy relationship success skills by being honest, trustworthy, loyal, concerned and responsible. Everybody makes mistakes and slips up. Lots of people value honesty, trust, loyalty, concern and responsibility but slip and take a fall into back into unhealthy, harmful behavior. Slipping on our values can lead to falling into harmful behavior. For example...

- Slipping on honesty by exaggerating can lead to falling back into lying.
- Slipping on trusting others by keeping things to yourself can lead to falling back into secret keeping about unhealthy, harmful behavior and staying by yourself.
- Slipping on being trustworthy by borrowing without asking can lead to falling back into stealing.
- Slipping on loyalty by not telling your partner who you are visiting can lead to falling into relationship cheating.
- Slipping on concern for yourself by hanging with negative peers can lead to falling back into unhealthy smoking, eating, drinking or drugging with them.
- Slipping on concern for others by dwelling on angry or arousing thoughts can lead to falling back into harmful physical or sexual behavior.
- Slipping on personal responsibility by not coming forward with mistakes can lead to falling back into blaming others.
- Slipping on social responsibility by not thinking about how your actions could affect others can lead to falling back into a "don't care" attitude and giving up on self-control.

Use the space below to write an example of how a slip in honesty, trust, loyalty, concern and responsibility led to taking a fall back into unhealthy, harmful behavior.

_____

_____

_____

_____

_____

In making mistakes and falling back into unhealthy, harmful behavior, how quickly you get back up is more important than how many mistakes you make. What really matters is how quickly you can get back on your feet and on back on the right track. Every minute you stay down is another minute you hurt yourself or others. Every minute you stand and stay on track with your values after a fall is another minute you reclaim your dignity through your honesty, trust, loyalty, concern and responsibility.

Breaking the Relapse Cycle

Correcting a slip to Avoid a Fall: The Olympic Ice Skater Example- In Olympic Ice Skating, a slip doesn't become a fall unless the skater hesitates in correcting it. If they are spinning when they land from a jump and slip but immediately extend their opposite arm, their fall turns into a graceful swoop narrowly touching the ice and recovering for the next jump. Only the judges know they slipped, the rest of us view it as a graceful swoop. Olympic Ice skaters make immediate moves to recover from slips as they are happening, they don't hesitate and as a result they rarely take a fall. The point here is simple, "Hesitation kills recovery"- If you hesitate in correcting a slip, you take a fall. Become a professional recovery Ice Skater. Learn to correct the Slip and avoid the Fall.

"You are only limited by your creativity" in coming up with ways to go to the opposite extreme [4] to correct a harmful behavior slip, break the relapse cycle and avoid taking a fall. Any ACTS skill (See pages 17- 27) that addresses a harmful behavior slip should be applied. "Avoid trouble", "Calm down" and "Think it through" are ACTS skills that are very useful in correcting a Slip to avoid a Fall.

"Avoid Trouble" with High Risk Situation Avoidance and Escape Skills

Dealing with high risk situations takes two basic types of skills. You need avoidance skills to help you identify high risk situations so you can avoid slipping into them and you need escape skills to get out of high risk situations when you have already slipped into them.

High Risk Situation Avoidance- List the last time you slipped into a high risk situation for harmful behavior relapse below. Then use positive planning and fantasy fast forward (p. 113) to point out how to correct that slip to avoid a fall back into harmful behavior.

Hint: Review your referral problem high risk situations and positive planning on p. 19- 20.

Last slip into a high risk situation- What was it and when? _____

_____

_____

High risk people- Who were they and why were they high risk to be around? _____

_____

High risk places- Where were you and why was that a high risk place to be in? _____

_____

Positive plan (to avoid high risk people and places)- _____

_____

_____

High risk feelings- What were they and how did they put you at risk for slipping into trouble?

_____

_____

Positive plan (to deal with these feelings)- _____

_____

_____

High risk thoughts- What were they and how did they put you at risk for slipping into trouble?

_____

_____

Positive plan (to manage these thoughts)- _____

_____

_____

Handling High Risk Thoughts: Responsible Self-statement Substitution 101

Irresponsible self-statements are things that you say to yourself that support unhealthy, harmful behavior. Responsible self-statements are things that you say to yourself that support healthy, helpful behavior and keeps you from falling back into harmful behavior. Responsible self-statement substitution is just learning how to identify irresponsible thinking (See Appendix C) and substitute responsible thinking. Doing this takes practice. Your Situation, Response, Analysis Log will help you learn to talk to yourself like your own best friend.

Use the following space to explain how you could use responsible self-statement substitution to help you change your irresponsible thinking in the following three situations. (If you are in a treatment group or have a therapist discuss this with them.)

Pay very close attention to justifying actions based on feelings, minimizing and blaming because these irresponsible thoughts are strong relapse triggers.

Explain what you need to do when you begin thinking about doing your problem behavior
What irresponsible thoughts will trigger going through with it?

_____

_____

_____

What responsible thoughts do you need to substitute to keep from going through with it?

_____

_____

_____

_____

Avoiding foresight slips into high risk situations- If we don't "keep our problem up front" and stay aware of our thoughts, feelings and situations, we are likely to make a foresight deficit decision and slip into a high risk situation for relapse. Describe the last foresight deficit decision that you made which caused you to slip into a high risk situation.

> **Hint:** A review of the foresight deficit decisions you described on p. 20- 21 and the examples in Appendix B (p. 110) including the description of fantasy fast forward (p. 113) should help.

Last Foresight Deficit Decision: I fell into a problem with _____

when I didn't think ahead about what could go wrong from _____

_____

Fantasy fast forward: If I think about being in a similar situation again and fast forward to the

end, I need to think ahead about _____

_____

and avoid trouble by _____

_____

High Risk Situation Escape- Use the three-Step Social Responsibility Plan (i.e., get out, get honest and get responsible) to escape trouble. Look at the high risk people, places and things that you listed in the previous section and describe how you could use your Three-step responsibility plan to escape those high risk situations and avoid falling into harmful behavior.

List the last high risk situation you slipped into here: _____

_____

Explain what you need to do in each of the three steps to escape that trouble if it occurs again. Discuss this with your therapist or group if you are in treatment.

Get out (Remove yourself). Leave the high risk situation without hesitation. What could you do

or say to get away from these people and out of these places? _____

_____

Get honest (Block irresponsible thinking by getting honest with yourself). What could happen

next if you don't stay out of that situation and how will you will feel later? _____

_____

Get responsible (Substitute more responsible thoughts). Replace the irresponsible thoughts that support entering or staying in high risk situations with responsible thoughts. Then substitute responsible thoughts. For example, "I need to stay out of that situation", "It's not worth the risk", "I need to put my recovery first" and escape trouble.

What I need to say to myself _____

What I need to do _____

Hint: What ACTS tools could you use to help you calm down?

Use the ABC's of Letting Feelings Go to Tolerate High Risk Emotions

Slipping into high risk emotions puts you at risk for justifying a harmful behavior based on unwanted feelings or old urges. Break your cycle by using the ABC's of Letting Feelings Go to keep from slipping into high risk emotions that set you up for relapse. Use the ABC's of Letting Feelings Go to relieve the unwanted feelings/urges that trigger slipping back into harmful behavior. Remember, "A" is the **A**ction that occurred (the problem situation or event); "B" is the **B**elief problem, about the action that works you up and triggers problem feelings or urges (i.e., often contains the word "should" or "must"); "C" is **C**hallenging the belief problem about the action to relieve the unwanted feeling/urge in order to prevent following that feeling into relapse (i.e., by Justifying Actions based on feelings, p. 124). High risk emotions can come from situations that meet our needs for attention, acceptance or excitement but at a price. We have to be very aware of these human needs and be careful not to compromise our recovery or endanger our freedom just to meet these needs. Some examples of using the ABC's of Letting Feelings Go to relieve the unwanted feelings/urges that trigger slipping back into harmful behavior are provided in Table 14 below.

Table 14.
Relieving high risk emotions: The ABC's of letting feelings go

Trust Abuse Action- A good looking person keeps flirting with me and my partner has been ignoring me. Belief- "I *should* go out with them just once. I deserve a little attention." (triggers excitement mixed with guilt over doing something behind their back) Challenging the belief to relieve stress- "Why should I make myself feel bad just for attention? I'm not falling into that." (lets go of need for attention and relieves guilt)
Substance abuse Action- I saw some friends getting high and they waived for me to come over and join them. Belief- "I *should* go over and visit. I haven't seen them since I got out of rehab." (triggers joy of seeing old friends followed by anxiety about violating probation for associating with using peers) Challenging the belief to relieve stress- "Where is the evidence that I must go over and visit? Meeting my needs for acceptance isn't worth a probation violation." (lets go of need for acceptance and relieves anxiety) **Food abuse** Action- I walked past a donut shop and got overwhelmed by the smell of fresh baked donuts. Belief- "I *must* buy donuts for my best friend who loves them and I'll only have one." (triggers anxiety over urge to break diet) Challenging the belief to relieve stress- "Why should I put myself at risk for relapse just to please someone else? I'm out of here! (lets go of anxiety over acting on urge).
Property Abuse Action- Someone left a wallet with money in the gym. Belief- "I *should* just keep it but what if there are cameras and I get caught?" (triggers excitement and anxiety over urge to steal) Challenging the belief to relieve stress- "How would I feel if it was mine and someone kept it? I'm turning it in." (lets go of acting on theft urge and relieves anxiety over getting caught)
Physical Abuse Action- A peer cursed at me in front of friends. Belief- "I *must* slap their mouth shut or people will think less of me." (triggers anger) Challenging the belief to relieve stress- "How likely is it that people will think less of me if I don't hit them but do speak up for myself? I'm not taking an assault charge for anyone's attitude problem. Protecting my freedom is more important than protecting my image." (lets go of acting on assault urge and relieves anger)
Sexual Abuse Action- I got drunk with a younger girl and she didn't say no when I came on to her. Belief- "She is too young but because she didn't say no this *must* mean yes it's OK to have sex with her." (triggers sexual excitement mixed with anxiety over doing something wrong) Challenging the belief to relieve stress- "Where is the evidence that not saying no, means yes? What if the worst happens and she changes her mind tomorrow when she sobers up? She's too young and I'm not compromising my freedom for me sexual excitement needs. I'm calling a cab to take her home." (lets go of acting on sexual urge relieves anxiety over doing something wrong)

"Think it Through" with the Reality Scales

Break your cycle by using the Reality Scales (rated on a 0- 10 scale) to "think though" how you handle high risk situations. List the last high risk situation for relapse (e.g., Person- running into someone who gets you thinking about it. Place- invitation to a party where slipping up was likely. Thing- feeling or thought that can lead to relapse) for relapse that you were faced with here.

Check whether you need to "think through" the decision to: enter these situations; stay in them if you already entered; return to them if you removed yourself or hold onto them if they are a thought or feeling. Then rate each one.

Survival scale- "How necessary for my survival is it for me to (check one- __enter, __stay in, __return to, __hold on to) this situation?" _____

(0 = not necessary; 10 = necessary to save my life)

Success scale- "How important is it to my success in life for me to (check one- __enter, __stay in, __return to, __hold on to) this situation?" _____

(0= not important at all; 10= so important I will never succeed in life without it)

Severity scale- "How severe could the consequences be if I (check one- __enter, __stay in, __return to, __hold on to) this situation?" _____ (0= not severe at all; 10= very severe)

Use the reality scale ratings above to "think though" the situation and write your responsible decision here- _____

_____

You can use the Reality Scales separately to weigh out your decision on whether or not to stay in a high risk situation, the Reality Scales are also useful in helping you "Get honest" on the second step of your three-step responsibility plan and "Challenge belief problems" in the ABC's of letting feelings go. For example...

Action- Strong feeling triggered by...
- smelling fresh baked cookies in the oven (high risk for unhealthy eating relapse)
- seeing peers getting high (high risk for substance abuse relapse)
- hearing someone cursing you and saying they will kick your ass (high risk for physical abuse relapse)
- seeing a peer changing out of their bathing suit after a pool party when everyone else already left (high risk for a sexual abuse relapse)

Belief- ("should" or "must") I can't stand this urge and *must* get these feelings off. If I don't act on these feelings [by eating drinking, drugging, slugging, spending or sex] my head will explode.

Challenge- Use reality scales to weigh out the truth that you can stand the feelings, they won't affect your survival or success in life if you don't follow them and not acting on them is not so severe that your head will explode.

Get honest about your Slips (lapses) with your therapist or treatment group. Log the date you discussed your Slips and how to Step Up to avoid them (see Exhibit 2, p. 105) along with who you discussed them with in the space provided below.

Date: _____ Discussed with: _____

The Stress-Relapse Cycle, Phase 5: Fall (or relapse)

"Failure is simply the opportunity to begin again, this time more intelligently"-- Henry Ford (1863- 1947)

Name: _____   **Date:** _____

Definition: A fall (or relapse) is a basic responsibility problem that involves giving up on our #1 social responsibility of self-control and falling back into harmful behavior. A fall involves indulging self and violating abstinence, goals or rules on any harmful behavior. For example: sexual abuse; physical abuse; property abuse (including gambling and overspending); substance abuse (including smoking cigarettes and overeating) and; trust abuse. In the final Phase of the Stress-Relapse Cycle, slipping continues until a fall back into harmful behavior occurs. When we let go of our #1 responsibility to maintain self-control and Fall back into harmful behavior, we are not protecting ourselves and others. A fall back into behavior that is harmful to ourselves is not protecting our health and fall back into behavior that is harmful to others is not only failing to protect the welfare of other it is also failing to protect our own freedom (i.e., can result in legal consequences).

Avoiding a Fall builds self-efficacy (confidence) which sets you up for future recovery success. Taking a Fall feeds "I can't" belief, feelings of helplessness, sets you up for another Fall. This moves your further away from being who you want to be and having the relationships you want by creating problems with honesty, trust, loyalty, concern and responsibility. The more we fall back into our old problem behavior, the less we uphold our number one responsibility of maintaining self-control. Breaking the Stress-Relapse Cycle requires a comprehensive individual relapse prevention plan that addresses the specific types of problems that each person has in each phase of their cycle: Negative Coping; Cover Up; Stress Buildup; Slip and; Fall.

Relapse Cycle Question # 5: What do you believe led you to fall back into your harmful behavior this last time?

Three basic Contributors to a Fall

There are many different ways that people Fall (relapse) back into harmful behavior. Three basic contributors to a Fall are: 1) Recovery Perfectionism; 2) Failure to Consider Consequences and; 3) Emotional Rumination.

Taking a Fall into Harmful Behavior through Recovery Perfectionism

Recovery Perfectionism involves not correcting a slip and taking a fall through "All or nothing" perfectionist thinking after making a mistake. Three types of Recovery Perfectionism thinking that result in giving up on self-control after a harmful behavior slip are referred to as the: "Abstinence violation effect" (Marlatt, 1985) when the slip violates abstinence from a harmful behavior (e.g., the slip breaks drug or alcohol abstinence); "Goal violation effect" (Larimer and Marlatt, 1990) when the slip violates a self-imposed personal goal (e.g., the slip breaks diet or exercise goals) and; "Rule violation effect" (Yokley, 2008) when the slip violates a rule (e.g., the slip breaks parole, probation or treatment program rules). Since harmful behavior creates desired feelings (e.g., sexual abuse) or gets rid of unwanted feelings (e.g., substance abuse), it is easy to make excuses, give up and fall back into it after a slip.

Recovery Perfectionism: The Slip Give Up Trigger

Allowing yourself to Slip creates self-disappointment and conflict with others that sets you up to give up. The "Slip Give Up Trigger" is the Recovery Perfectionism chain of events which occurs in the abstinence, goal and rule violation effect involving a slip and then giving up. Giving up is related to recovery perfectionism and "I can't" belief followed by justifying actions of continuing harmful behavior based on feelings of self-disappointment or helplessness. Taking a Fall through the Slip Give Up Trigger involves the following basic steps. "Since I slipped and broke my [sobriety, promise, goal or parole], I completely blew it and can't turn things around so I might as well just give up [on self-control] and keep going. Besides, if I stop now, there will still be consequences." [having to tell my AA sponsor/group, apologize, start my goal over, get a parole violation hearing]. In short, "I blew it so screw it, I give up" (on self-control). Table 15 below provides examples of how recovery perfectionism results in relapse through the slip give up trigger across multiple forms of harmful behavior.

Table 15.
Slip Give Up Trigger Examples across Harmful Behaviors

Example	Since I already slipped and…	I blew it so I might as well just…	Besides, if I stop now, I will…
Trust Abuse	gave them my number	cheat [**give up** on couples therapy]	not be able to get it off my mind
Substance Abuse (including cigarettes, food)	had one: sip, hit, snort, shot, line, smoke, drag, bite, etc.	keep going [**give up** on AA, NA, CA, OA, smoke-enders, etc.]	still have to start my recovery program over
Property Abuse	put it in my pocket	leave the store with it [**give up** on probation]	get caught putting it back
Physical Abuse	threatened them	beat their ass [**give up** on anger management]	have to take their crap
Sexual Abuse	was seen alone with a child	get sex [**give up** on SO treatment]	still get a parole violation

One type of Harmful Behavior can Trigger Another

The same "all or nothing" Recovery Perfectionism thinking that occurs within harmful behavior treatment when trying to maintain abstinence, goals or rules, i.e., "Since I already slipped and blew my [sexual, physical, property, substance or trust abuse] treatment plan, I might as well just give up keep going" (See Table 15) can occur between harmful behaviors. For example...

• "Since I've already overcharged my credit card (trust abuse), I might as well go out drinking on it (triggers substance abuse). Besides, if I stop now I'm still not going to be able to pay and will get a late charge anyway."
• "Since I already got high and flirted with a friend (substance abuse), I might as well cheat on my partner. Besides, if I stop now it will look like I did anyway (triggers trust abuse)."
• "Since I already stole from them (property abuse), I might as well use the money to get high (triggers harmful behavior)."

- "Since I already fondled them (sexual abuse), I might as well threaten beat and them (triggers physical abuse) to see if I can keep them from telling."

Taking a Fall into Harmful Behavior through Failure to Consider Consequences
"If you're not working on the solution, you're part of the problem" [1]
Taking a fall into harmful behavior can occur through failure to consider the consequences of: 1) the emotional, physical and legal impact of the harmful behavior and; 2) continued access to high risk situations for relapse.

Failure to Consider the Emotional, Physical and Consequences of Harmful Behavior
A summary of the typical emotional, physical and legal consequences of taking a fall into harmful behavior is provided in Table 16 below. Since harmful behavior can result in serious consequences to self and others, mentally blocking out awareness of those consequences is a typical defensive reaction. Blocking out awareness of the consequences of harmful behavior includes: Minimizing consequences, e.g., "It's not so bad", "No one ever dies from this"; "Normalizing" the behavior (e.g., "lots of people do it") often by hanging out with people who do the behavior, approve of it or have worse problems and; Justifying, e.g., "I deserve it, I've earned it" or "They deserve it after what they did". Grandiosity or super-optimism (Yochelson and Samenow, 1977) also acts to block out awareness of consequences, e.g., "I don't need to make relapse prevention plans to avoid these [people, places, things], I can handle it", "Nothing will happen", "No one will find out and if they do, am always able to talk my way out of whatever happens."

Table 16. Typical Consequences of Taking a Fall into Harmful Behavior

Harmful Behavior	Consequences to Self	Consequences to Others
Trust Abuse Substance Abuse Property Abuse Physical Abuse Sexual Abuse	**Emotional problems**- Depression, anxiety or anger from separation, divorce, job loss, friendship loss. Fear of violence from those who were harmed. **Physical problems**- HIV, Hepatitis C, STD's Harmful weight gain or loss. **Legal problems**- "Freedom suicide"- jail for DUI: vehicular homicide; stealing; dealing; physical or sexual assault	Victims of harmful behavior suffer severe... **Emotional problems**- Depression, anxiety or anger. **Physical problems**- Severe injury or death as a result of MVA, physical or sexual assault, infection with HIV, Hepatitis C, STD's **Legal problems**- Medical bills, legal bills, funeral costs

Failure to Consider Consequences of Continued Access to high risk situations
The top three most important things in selling a house are location, location and location while the top three most important things in harmful behavior relapse are access, access and access. Continued access to high risk people, places or things increases the probability of dwelling on the expected benefit from doing the behavior (e.g., desired feelings) or dwelling on expected relief (i.e., from an undesirable situation or unwanted feelings) after doing the behavior. Continued access to high risk people eventually results in relapse due to an urge triggered by talking to or seeing someone you could do the behavior with (e.g., fellow druggies, drinkers, smokers, foodies- negative social influence) or to (e.g., potential victims of sexual, physical, property or trust abuse/conning). Continued access to high risk places eventually results in

relapse due to opportunity such as isolation where there are no witnesses, places where you have done it before or places where others are doing the behavior (e.g., parties, bars, casinos, brothels). Continued access to high risk things (e.g., junk food, cigarettes, drugs, alcohol, porno, weapons) provides the means to relapse into harmful behavior.

Falling back into Harmful Behavior through Emotional Rumination

Rumination is going over and over a thought in your mind, dwelling on it and not letting it go. To ruminate means "to chew over again" and is based on the physical behavior of cows who ruminate their food by spitting it up and chewing on it some more. Humans do the same thing with thoughts, they bring up old thoughts and chew on them some more. This is why grandma used to say… "You need to stop chewing on that" (meaning let it go). Cows ruminate to further digest their food but when humans ruminate on thoughts they often get worked up into a negative feeling and end up doing something wrong as opposed to solving the problem

Since "there are only two things you can't change in life, the past and other people's behavior", rumination on the past and other people's behavior often results in feelings of helplessness and other unwanted emotions that set the occasion for relapse. For example, rumination on…

- Past mistakes often results in self-pity, "I can't" belief giving up on self-control.
- Past problems often results in anxiety, depression and escape (e.g., eating, drinking, smoking, sex, etc).
- Past injustices often results in anger, resentment and revenge (i.e., getting even).
- Past partner flirting often results in insecurity, jealousy, anger and aggression relapse (e.g., domestic violence).
- Past partying (euphoric recall) often results in harmful behavior cravings and relapse urges.
- Past sexual fantasies often results in sexual behavior planning.
- Other people's behavior, their mistakes, their attitude towards you results in unwanted feelings and the urge to vent them in harmful ways.

Isolation, loneliness and boredom sets you up to work yourself up by dwelling on the pleasurable feeling the harmful behavior will bring or the relief from unwanted feelings that the behavior will bring. Think about it, the brain is a three pound problem solving machine bolted to your shoulders. When you are alone and doing nothing, the brain does not start going over that time you went to Disney World or any other positive past event because those are not problems. What happens is your brain pulls the next unsolved problem off the shelf and starts working on it. Ruminating on past problems makes depression, anxiety and anger worse, especially if those problems have to do with things that you can't change such as the past or other people's behavior. Here's the bad part. If the problem is hard to solve or impossible to solve you can get angry, anxious or depressed. This leads the brain into problem solving how to get rid of the unwanted feeling and dwelling on relapse (e.g., harmful eating, drinking, drugging, slugging, spending, sex, etc.) to get pleasurable feelings or avoid painful ones. Emotional rumination justifies relapse in two basic ways:

1. The pursuit of pleasure (sensation seeking)- Working self up dwelling on the pleasurable sensation that doing the behavior will bring, and staying stuck on that feeling by ruminating

on thoughts about the thrill, rush, high, power trip or pleasurable feeling you can get from the behavior ("euphoric recall" or telling "war stories" doing the behavior).

OR

2. The avoidance of pain (relief seeking)- Working self up dwelling on the relief from unwanted thoughts or feelings the behavior will bring (focusing on avoiding pain and seeking relief) and staying stuck on that feeling by ruminating on getting relief or comfort from the behavior. Relief seeking includes magnifying the severity of the unwanted situation in order to justify the need for relief by doing the behavior.

When a Fall involves ruminating on behavior designed to alter your mood either by the pursuit of pleasure or avoidance of pain, common motives are: 1) building yourself up by putting others down in order to relieve inadequacy or feel superior; 2) gratifying your urges to get high, smoke, overeat or achieve an orgasm in order to relieve an undesired mood or produce a desired mood; 3) hurting or manipulating others to feel in control or get high on power or revenge; 4) doing illegal, risky or harmful behaviors to break boredom, fulfill an exaggerated need for attention, excitement or thrill seeking and; 5) compromising yourself to be accepted or feel needed by doing things against your better judgment or forgetting about yourself altogether and focusing all of your concern on others. Relapse behavior by gratifying your impulses produces a temporary increase of the desired mood or temporary relief from the undesired mood either of which may make you temporarily feel in control. A summary of emotional rumination across harmful behaviors is provided in Table 17.

Table 17
Emotional Rumination: Summary Across Harmful Behaviors

Harmful Behavior	Sensation Seeking	Relief Seeking
Trust Abuse	Seeking attention, acceptance or excitement, lying to impress or entertain others	Seeking to relieve fear, lying to avoid consequences
Food Abuse	Seeking a satisfying holiday meal with relatives	Seeking to relieve stress by comfort eating
Substance Abuse	Seeking a good time high, partying with friends	Seeking to relieve unwanted feelings (social anxiety, depression from loss, anger over injustice)
Property Abuse	Seeking a thrill crime high, shoplifting, auto theft	Seeking to relieve stress, get anger off through vandalism
Physical Abuse	Seeking feelings of control and power	Seeking relief of past hurt through revenge
Sexual Abuse	Seeking a sexual high, partying with prostitutes, dangerous sex, sex with minors	Seeking relief from break up depression, using someone for rebound relationship sex. Wanting support and mistaking intensity for intimacy.

Please mark the following scales below so that we can see how aware you are of the types of Falls (relapses) that were involved in your Stress-Relapse Cycle.

A. Use the numbers on the rating scale below to indicate how often you have taken a Fall back into (or relapsed on) **the following unhealthy, harmful behaviors that were harmful to yourself or others.**

0 Never	1 Once	2 A Few Times	3 Often	4 Very Frequently

____ 1) Alcohol abuse which endangered yourself?

____ 2) Tobacco abuse which endangered yourself (e.g., created a health problem or made an existing health problem worse)?

____ 3) Tobacco abuse which endangered others (e.g., falling asleep while smoking, smoking in bed or other situation that could create a fire hazard)?

____ 4) Alcohol abuse which endangered, abused or violated the rights of others (e.g., caused an auto accident, got intoxicated and disorderly, threatened violence to others, caused harm to others or their property, got charged with domestic violence, assaulted someone while intoxicated, got charged with driving while intoxicated, committed a theft or robbery while intoxicated or to get money for substance abuse)?

____ 5) Drug abuse which endangered yourself?

____ 6) Drug abuse which endangered, abused or violated the rights of others (e.g., caused an auto accident, got intoxicated and disorderly, threatened violence to others, caused harm to others or their property, got charged with domestic violence, assaulted someone while intoxicated, got charged with driving while intoxicated, committed a theft or robbery while intoxicated or to get money for substance abuse)?

____ 7) Prescription drug abuse (e.g., Valium, pain killers, etc.) which endangered yourself?

____ 8) Prescription drug abuse (e.g., Valium, pain killers, etc.) which endangered, abused or violated the rights of others (e.g., caused an auto accident, got intoxicated and disorderly, threatened violence to others, caused harm to others or their property, got charged with domestic violence, assaulted someone while intoxicated, got charged with driving while intoxicated, committed a theft or robbery while intoxicated or to get money for substance abuse)?

____ 9) Food abuse (e.g., long term over eating, short term food binges, purging or starving self)?

____10) Responsibility neglect- Letting your responsibilities go and just doing what you want, what is easiest, what you feel like doing or what makes you feel good at the time (Youth example- making excuses to miss or skip school/work, not completing activities that are required of you; Adult example- failure to pay bills or being an absent parent to your children)?

____11) Responsibility abuse- Refusal to accept your responsibilities (Includes irresponsible behavior, for example quitting school or job training, quitting a job without getting another job first. Also includes pathological priorities, for example as a parent putting involvement in adult relationships/activities before family/child care needs)?

Use the numbers on the rating scale below to indicate how often you have taken a Fall back into (or relapsed on) the following unhealthy, harmful behaviors.

0	1	2	3	4
Never	Once	A Few Times	Often	Very Frequently

___12) Responsibility overdose- Falling into becoming responsible for everyone and everything all the time, resulting in burnout and resentment from others always calling on you to get things done or help them out but not returning the favor?

___13) Money abuse (e.g., compulsive gambling, chronic irresponsible spending, compulsive spending or shopaholic, excess credit card debt)?

___14) Loyalty neglect such as: walking out on a friend in need; shifting your loyalties to others when it seems to benefit you or when things aren't going well for your current friends or; putting associates before family?

___15) Loyalty abuse- Ignoring long time friends and showing favoritism to associates who are more attractive and popular or as a parent by spending more time with one child than another?

___16) Trust abuse (i.e., abusing the trust of others by lying, deceiving, manipulating, conning, etc., including cheating on a partner or having an intimate relationship with more than one person while telling them both what they want to hear)?

___17) Falling back into an unhealthy relationship (e.g., following feelings, picking looks over loyalty and being cheated on or picking companionship over concern and being mistreated)?

___18) Falling into rapid relationship involvement or "rebound" relationships after breakups to avoid loneliness, emptiness or feeling unwanted and being disappointed again?

___19) Concern/emotional abuse of others, e.g., putting others down to build yourself up or being cruel and hurting others emotionally to get power over them or to win a sick argument?

___20) Concern/emotional neglect of self, e.g., putting others first to the point of getting totally involved in doing for them and forgetting about self and own needs or falling back into a relationship where you put more in than you get back?

___21) Power abuse (i.e., using your position of status, popularity or power to get others to do what you want- winning by intimidation, controlling/dominating)?

___22) Emotional neglect (e.g., refusal to offer comfort and support to another person that you can see is hurting and needs help or giving those who care about you the "silent treatment")?

___23) Physical neglect (e.g., not sharing when asked or not giving something that you don't really need to someone who needs it more)?

Use the numbers on the rating scale below to indicate how often you have taken a Fall back into (or relapsed on) the following unhealthy, harmful behaviors.

0	1	2	3	4
Never	**Once**	**A Few Times**	**Often**	**Very Frequently**

____24) Taken advantage of someone's weakness to get your own way?

____25) Verbal abuse (e.g., menacing or threats of violence- to hit, beat up, stab, shoot, kill- with severe temper, rageoholic)?

____26) Property abuse (i.e., stealing from others, borrowing and not returning things, breaking things and not replacing them, breaking things on purpose, vandalism)?

____27) Physical abuse or assault (e.g., held down, pushed, shoved, slapped, hit, stabbed, shot someone- including hitting, slapping a partner during arguments- also includes conviction on domestic violence or disorderly conduct from fighting and ongoing school bullying)?

____28) Sexual abuse of someone your age or an adult (e.g., coerced or forced them into sexual acts or got them drunk/high so you could take advantage of them sexually or getting others to prostitute themselves)?

____29) Sexual abuse of a child (i.e., had any type of sexual contact with children under age 13 or sexual contact with someone under age 18 who was 5 or more years younger than yourself)?

____30) Sexual acting out (e.g., compulsive unprotected sex, pornography use, promiscuity, prostitution, phone or internet sex)?

____31) Homicide or homicide attempt (violent assault with intent to kill)?

32) What other forms of unhealthy, harmful behavior have you slipped and fallen into? Discuss your past problems with your treatment group and/or therapist. Include their feedback.

_____

As mentioned at the beginning of this section, taking a Fall (or relapse) can be the result of: an irresponsible release of stress build-up; altering your mood or; the rule violation effect.

B. Use the numbers on the rating scale below to indicate how often to you believe the falls you have taken back into your harmful behavior (relapse) in section A above has related to the following causes.

0	1	2	3	4
Never	**Once**	**A Few Times**	**Often**	**Very Frequently**

How often do you feel that your Fall into harmful behavior has related to...

____ 1) an irresponsible release of Stress Build-Up (i.e., avoiding getting honest and dealing with problems by letting stress from self-disappointment along with worry about getting caught come to a boil and get acted out)?

Use the numbers on the rating scale below to indicate how often to you believe the falls you have taken back into your harmful behavior in section A above has related to the following causes.

0	1	2	3	4
Never	**Once**	**A Few Times**	**Often**	**Very Frequently**

How often do you feel that your Fall into harmful behavior has related to...

____ 2) using substances (e.g., drugs/alcohol, tobacco, food), people (e.g., manipulating, controlling or dominating others physically or sexually) or exciting things (e.g., thrill activities or risky, exciting behaviors to break boredom, fulfill an exaggerated need for excitement or get a thrill)?

____ 3) following feelings and not thinking things through, justifying actions based on feelings?

____ 4) telling yourself there's no use in trying, you just can't do it?

____ 5) doing things you shouldn't to fit in or be accepted?

____ 6) letting teasing, joking or horseplay go too far?

____ 7) doing things you shouldn't for attention?

____ 8) working self up emotionally, then losing control?

____ 9) keeping score and getting even (revenge)?

____ 10) The Rule violation effect? (see examples below)

Examples of the "Slip Give Up Trigger" (AKA rule violation effect) for substance abusers (of a. alcohol, b. tobacco products and c. food), trust abusers (of d. relationships, e. money and f. property) and people abusers (g. physically and h. sexually) are listed below.

"Since I've already slipped and...	a. had a sip of beer, b. smoked a cigarette, c. tasted a donut, d. gone out date with someone else,	e. used my overextended credit card f. borrowed from the cash register, g. gotten mad & yelled threats, h. isolated a child,
I might as well give up and...	a. finish the six pack. b. finish the pack. c. finish the box. d. cheat on my wife.	e. make a bet to try & break even f. keep it. g. kick their ass. h. have sex with them.
Why not, I already...	a. blew my recovery time. b. broke my promise. c. broke my diet. d. broke my commitment.	e. got in trouble with the bank f. broke the rules. g. verbally assaulted them. h. violated my parole.
Besides, I've got to...	a. start my recovery over again b. feel bad about letting my family down anyway c. start my diet over d. lie to my partner anyway	e. lie about what I did anyway f. deny it anyway g. teach them a lesson and make them respect me anyway h. worry about getting caught anyway
and the consequences of continuing probably won't be any more than if I stop right now because everyone always assumes the worst."		

Please list any personal rule violation effect example you can recall (Use the workspace on page 99 if needed)

_____

_____

_____

Initiate a discussion with your treatment group or therapist on your top reasons for taking a Fall record those reasons and the date you completed this discussion here→ _____

_____

_____

C. Review the relapse ratings that you marked in section A above. Then list the top three most frequent harmful behavior relapse problems that you had in the PAST (i.e., before you began to receive treatment for your harmful behavior) **in the space provided below.**

<u>**Make sure that your referral form of harmful behavior is included and listed first**</u>.
Top Three Most Frequent PAST harmful behavior Relapse Problems (before entering treatment)

1) Harmful behavior that was the reason for referral-_____

It has been _____ (list years, months and weeks) since the last time I was involved in the above type of harmful behavior and I believe that I am at:
(___Low; ___Moderate or; ___ High) risk for relapse on the above type of harmful behavior.

2) _____

It has been _____ (list years, months and weeks) since the last time I was involved in the above type of harmful behavior and I believe that I am at:
(___Low; ___Moderate or; ___ High) risk for relapse on the above type of harmful behavior.

3) _____

It has been _____ (list years, months and weeks) since the last time I was involved in the above type of harmful behavior and I believe that I am at:
(___Low; ___Moderate or; ___ High) risk for relapse on the above type of harmful behavior.

D. Go back through the questions in Section A above. Then circle the ratings of those behaviors that you have exhibited in the PRESENT (i.e., after you began to receive treatment for your harmful behavior).

E. Review the PRESENT relapse ratings that you circled in Section A above. Then list the top three most frequent PRESENT harmful behavior relapse problems in the spaces provided below.

Top Three Most Frequent PRESENT Harmful behavior Relapse Problems (after entering treatment)

1) _____

It has been _____ (list months, weeks and days) since the last time I was involved in the above type of harmful behavior and I believe that I am at:

(___Low; ___Moderate or; ___ High) risk for relapse on the above type of harmful behavior.

2) _____

It has been _____ (list months, weeks and days) since the last time I was involved in the above type of harmful behavior and I believe that I am at:

(___Low; ___Moderate or; ___ High) risk for relapse on the above type of harmful behavior.

3) _____

It has been _____ (list months, weeks and days) since the last time I was involved in the above type of harmful behavior and I believe that I am at:

(___Low; ___Moderate or; ___ High) risk for relapse on the above type of harmful behavior.

F. **Review your answers to the questions above and record at least the top three most frequent PRESENT** (i.e., your referral problem behavior and other harmful behaviors that you were doing) **and PAST harmful behavior Falls that you took on the Stress-Relapse Cycle worksheet (page 101).** Place the most frequent type first, the second most frequent second, etc. Make sure to include your referral form of harmful behavior first on your list. Discuss this with your therapist or group. Note: If the harmful behavior that resulted in your treatment referral has gone on long enough so that you have a number of relapse episodes or harmful behavior victims, use all of the space on the cycle worksheet to list your treatment referral relapse episodes. For example, with food abuse relapse, list names of all of the diet and exercise programs that you tried but relapsed into overeating after completion. With drug/alcohol relapse, list treatment program names, re-arrests or probation/parole violations. With interpersonal abuse (e.g., physical or sexual abuse), list victim first names whenever possible.

Summary Completion Instructions- Imagine yourself teaching someone else about this part of your life. Put your important descriptions in phrase form that makes it easy for you to explain and makes sense when read by others. Don't limit yourself to the top three points if there are important parts that fit in this area. Make sure that you do not leave out any important information about yourself on this topic. Use the margins if needed.

G. **Update your relapse prevention plan if you have completed workbook 1. If you haven't completed workbook #1, make a relapse prevention plan** with your therapist or treatment staff for your referral form of harmful behavior (behavior that resulted in your treatment referral) based on what you have learned from this workbook about your harmful behavior and what you can do to avoid falling back into your Stress-Relapse Cycle.

In either case, be sure to cover:

1. <u>Cognitive Risk Factors</u> including types of Negative Coping that could set you up for relapse;
2. <u>Situational Risk Factors</u> including types of Cover Up that could build up stress and lead to relapse and;
3. <u>Social-Emotional Risk Factors</u> including types of Stress Build-Up and Slips/Lapses that could set you up for relapse.

"Nothing succeeds like success". Your healthy pride, self-efficacy and social maturity will improve each time that you **Recover** from your relapse urges and uphold your social responsibility to help yourself and others through appropriate social behavior control.

H. Update your promise letter if you have completed workbook 1. If you haven't completed workbook #1, write a promise letter. Start with "Dear (list those you have let down and yourself if you have suffered from the harmful behavior)", and continue with something to the effect of- "I am making a commitment to stop (the unhealthy, harmful behavior) that led to my need for treatment. Be sure to add "I have learned about how I maintained this problem through a Stress-Relapse" and explain what you have learned from this workbook. Add important Stress-Relapse Cycle information that you are going to use in your relapse prevention and commitment to change.

"Two heads are better than one, four eyes are better than two". Discuss your relapse prevention plan and promise letter with your therapist and treatment group. In all of your Social Responsibility Therapy discussions, use the "<u>Window Concept</u>" to help you decide what to apply and the "<u>Mirror Concept</u>" to help you accept and benefit most from what applies. The "Window Concept" involves keeping the window open by keeping an open mind, taking in everything everyone tells you and examining it carefully. If it is helpful to yourself or others hold it dear to your heart, if it's not, shovel it out the window. If there is any doubt about whether to keep and apply the feedback you receive, use group consensus (i.e., "If ten people say you're a horse, you're a horse"). The "Mirror Concept" is accepting that that "other people see you better than you see yourself" and you need to use their feedback as a mirror to get a better view of yourself.

The ART of Social Responsibility Therapy: Breaking a Fall [9]

Taking Fall is a Responsibility Problem involving giving up on our #1 social responsibility of self-control and falling back into harmful behavior. "You are only limited by your creativity" in coming up with opposite extreme[4] ways to break the stress-relapse cycle and stop a fall back into harmful behavior. Any ACTS skill (i.e., Avoid trouble, Calm down, Think it through and Solve the problem) that helps avoid a fall back into harmful behavior should be applied. The following are some brief examples of how to apply ACTS healthy behavior success skills to break a fall from: Recovery Perfectionism; Failure to Consider Consequences and; Emotional Rumination.

Breaking a Fall from Recovery Perfectionism

Examples of how to stop recovery perfectionism (i.e., being a perfectionist with recovery and giving up after a minor mistake) and break a fall by interrupting the Slip Give Up Trigger that results in relapse are provided in Table 18.

Table 18.
Blocking the Slip Give Up Trigger and Breaking a Fall

Taking a Fall	Breaking a Fall
Since I already slipped and broke my [sobriety, promise, goal or parole]	Admit that a Slip doesn't become a Fall unless you hesitate in correcting it.
I completely blew it [recovery perfectionism]	Be a recovery Ice Skater, take immediate action during slips to avoid a fall.
and can't turn things around so I might as well just give up and keep going ["I can't" belief]	Admit that the only way to guarantee you can't turn things around is to give up. Then step up your recovery effort.
Besides, if I stop now, there will still be consequences [justifying continuing]	Use the reality scales to weigh the consequences of stopping against continuing

Complete the exercise below to show that you understand recovery perfectionism and how the Slip Give Up Trigger results in relapse. Break down how one of your past slips led to a fall though the Slip Give Up Trigger by completing the following.

"Since I slipped and..." _____

"I completely blew it and can't turn things around so I might as well just..." _____

_____

_____

"Besides, if I stop now I will..." _____

_____

_____

Describe what you could say to yourself or do to stop the slip give up trigger and keep from

falling into harmful behavior. _____

_____

_____

Breaking a Fall from Failure to Consider Consequences

Failure to Consider the Emotional, Physical and Consequences of Harmful Behavior

List your referral problem (i.e., the harmful behavior that resulted in a referral for treatment)

here _____

Describe the possible consequences of the harmful behavior you listed above in the boxes below.

Type of Consequences	Consequences to Self	Consequences to Others
Emotional problems-		
Physical problems-		
Legal problems-		

Life Impact Statement: The Stress-Relapse Cycle

Use the space below to record how repeating the harmful behavior that resulted in your referral for treatment has affected your life. Begin by recording the number of times you have relapsed or repeated your problem below. For example, with problems that are primarily harmful to self (upper left section of Table 1), if you are in an obesity treatment program for severe weight gain that is harmful to your health, record your worst weight along with the number and type of diets or exercise programs that you have tried. Regarding problems that are harmful to self and others (center section of Table 1), if you are in a substance abuse treatment program for a severe drinking problem that has become harmful to yourself and others, record the serious consequences to yourself (e.g., liver damage and drunk driving criminal record) and others (i.e., record the harmful impact of your worst episode) along with the number and names of the people you have harmed and how they were harmed. Regarding problems that are primarily harmful to others (lower right section of Table 1), if you are in a sex offender treatment program for a sexual behavior problem that has become harmful to others, record the harmful impact of your worst episode along with the number and names of the victims that you have harmed. In all cases list the treatment programs that you have tried, the number of years you have been struggling with the harmful behavior problem and any social or legal consequences that you have experienced as a result of that problem. Use the workspace on page 99 if needed.

_____

_____

_____

_____

_____

_____

_____

_____

_____

_____

_____

_____

_____

_____

_____

_____

_____

_____

_____

_____

_____

_____

Protect the rights of others, protect your freedom and protect your health starting by focusing on the possible consequences of your decision before taking action. Do a Reality Check. Ask yourself, "Is what I'm considering helpful or harmful to myself and others?"

Irresponsible Thinking Problem: Failure to consider consequences of Emotional, Physical and Consequences of Harmful Behavior is supported by Minimizing, Normalizing and Justifying the behavior along with Grandiosity Planning Problems.

   Minimizing Solution: Go to the opposite extreme in your imagination and get honest with yourself about the worst case scenario. "What is the worst that could happen?" both now and in the long run.

   Normalizing Solution: "Keep your problem up front" and go to the opposite extreme of social normalizing by hanging with those who are against, do not engage in or approve of the harmful behavior. "Take a position with yourself" and put yourself in social situations where it will be difficult if not impossible to relapse. Gather the courage to make opposite extreme friends.

   Justifying Solution: Be responsible to yourself and others. Don't let stress buildup until you blow up (relapse). If you earned something give yourself credit not consequences, tell your accomplishment to someone who cares about you. If someone deserves a consequence, don't get caught up in getting even which could end up hurting you. Accept that "The best revenge is success" and do something positive for you, not negative to them.

   Grandiosity Solution: Get real, admit that telling yourself "I can handle it" and staying in high risk situations sets you up for a fall. Accept that "Planning power beats willpower" and if you don't think ahead, you earn the consequences of whatever goes wrong. "Accidents happen, behaviors are planned and consequences are earned". Do a Reality Check, ask yourself "Is what I'm considering helpful or harmful to myself and others?" Then use positive planning, "Think ahead, plan ahead, get ahead". The reality check is referred to as the "window concept" in the therapeutic community where residents are told, "If it's helpful to yourself or others keep the idea, if not, shovel it out the window." Learn to tolerate waiting to take action by getting honest with yourself that, "I can always do this later" and getting an opinion from a trusted responsible other on the chances that there will be consequences to yourself or others.

Failure to Consider Consequences of Continued Access to high risk situations

Read the definition of "Fantasy Fast Forward" on p. 113 and then describe the possible consequences of staying in high risk situations in the boxes below.

High Risk Situation	Consequences to Self (Use Fantasy Fast Forward)	Consequences to Others (Use Fantasy Fast Forward)
List High Risk People here...	What could happen if I hang out with them-	What could happen if I hang out with them-

High Risk Situation	Consequences to Self (Use Fantasy Fast Forward)	Consequences to Others (Use Fantasy Fast Forward)
List High Risk Places here...	What could happen if I don't get out-	What could happen if I don't get out-
List High Risk Feelings here...	What could happen if I don't let feelings go-	What could happen if I don't let feelings go-
List High Risk Thoughts here... (Appendix C, p. 114)	What could happen if I don't substitute responsible thoughts-	What could happen if I don't substitute responsible thoughts-

High Risk Situation Problem: Staying in high risk situations that maintain access to and thoughts about and trigger feelings or urges to do the harmful behavior sets you up for failure. **Solution**: "Keep your problem up front" and go to the opposite extreme by getting out and staying out of places where your harmful behavior is likely using the three-step social responsibility plan. Set yourself up to succeed by Going to the opposite extreme and set up the physical environment you live in for success. Develop a "sanctuary" home that makes recovery convenient and relapse inconvenient. "Win the war outside the door"- Don't bring home junk food, cigarettes, alcohol, drugs, porno or negative, enabling friends. If you have to see enabling friends, don't invite them over. If there is some extremely important reason you have to see them, meet at a restaurant so you can use the three step social responsibility plan to escape if needed.

Breaking a Fall from Emotional Rumination
Humans have basic needs for attention, acceptance and excitement. We don't really like to be ignored, rejected or bored. We all have these needs and only differ in how much of each that we have. Use the scales below to rate your level of each of these basic human needs.

Attention Needs (0- 10) _____

    0 = Don't like attention at all. I would rather be ignored and left by myself.

    10 = Very strong need for attention, upset if I don't get recognized for doing something good.

Acceptance Needs (0- 10) _____

    0= No need for acceptance at all. Rejection never bothers me. I have a strong history of acceptance from positive parents, partners and peers who don't have harmful behavior.

    10= Strong need for acceptance. Rejection is always hard for me to handle. I have a past history of rejection from parents, partners or peers.

Excitement Needs (0- 10) _____

    0= No need for excitement at all. Boredom never bothers me. I don't need anything to do.

    10= Strong need for excitement. I can't stand being bored. I like to do exciting things.

Emotional Rumination: "Relapse is not the problem; it's a poor solution to the problem"

Falling Back into the Stress-Relapse Cycle. My harmful behavior gave me (check one):

___1) pleasurable, good feelings, a high, power boost or increase in confidence/control

___2) relief or distraction from unwanted feelings or thoughts

___3) both #1 and #2

___4) other (_____)

Why is it important to know what you get from your unhealthy, harmful behavior?

_____

_____

Stopping Emotional Rumination on the Pursuit of Pleasure (Sensation Seeking)

Using harmful behavior sensation seeking (e.g., excessive partying, risky sex, thrill crimes, control and power trips) as a distraction to avoid dealing with life problems is a poor solution to the problem. Not only is sensation seeking a poor solution because you have to pay in both cash and consequences, it is also a poor solution because it is temporarily and will wear off. The problem with sensation seeking is that as soon as the thrill is gone, the depression, anxiety or other feelings related to life problems returns. Since this sets the occasion for relapse back into sensation seeking harmful behavior, "Relapse is not the problem; it's a poor solution to the problem". If you don't think you are sensation seeking to distract yourself from dealing with unwanted feelings or serious life problems and feel, "I just do it because I like it", chances are that you have a low tolerance for boredom and a strong need for excitement. If this is the case you need to: learn how to let those feelings go; find exciting activities that are positive; learn boredom tolerance (i.e., beginning with admitting that "if you're bored, you're boring because you can't think of any positive exciting things to do"); "get paid, not played" and; develop the courage to try new positive exciting things. For example, think about meeting needs for excitement with a positive occupation such as sky diving instructor, race car driver, competitive sports, policeman, fireman or military special operations where you get paid for an exciting career. Complete the exercise below to show how you can use the ABC's of letting feelings go in a situation that triggers a sensation seeking relapse urge.

Action that occurred (the problem situation or event). Imagine that your need for excitement gets triggered by the opportunity to do a harmful behavior and you start ruminating on the pleasurable feeling you will get from that behavior. Describe a situation where that could happen to you.

_____

_____

_____

Belief problem about the action that triggers the sensation seeking relapse urge (i.e., often contains the word "should" or "must"). For example, "I _must_ have my needs met and can't stand it if I don't."

_____

_____

_____

Challenging the words "should" or "must" that support the belief problem to relieve stress buildup by letting feelings go. For example, "Where is the evidence that I must have my needs met? Unmet needs can't stop my heart and breathing so I can stand it, it's an urge not an order."

_____

_____

_____

Preoccupation with pleasure- Working self up dwelling on the pleasurable feeling the problem behavior creates a "tunnel vision" focus only on benefits, you can get from the behavior, blocks considering consequences. Impairs foresight and prevents role reversal, "failure to put self in the place of others" is a social responsibility problem which allows relapse. "Be your brother's keeper" by using past experiences and fantasy fast forward (see p. 113) to consider what could happen to self and others. Admit that when we do harmful things to ourselves, it hurts those who care about us and when we do harmful things to others, the consequences end up hurting us. Use the decisional balance reality scales to weigh the benefits against the consequences to self/others of pleasurable but harmful behaviors. In addition, for the long term decision on whether to continue meeting needs for excitement through harmful behavior or find a positive way to meet excitement needs, use the following reality scales to weigh out your decision on how to best meet your needs for excitement.

Survival scale-

How necessary for my survival is it for me to...	
Continue harmful activities that are exciting? (e.g., excessive partying, risky sex or thrill crimes, etc.)	Develop exciting activities that are not harmful? (e.g., enter an exciting career in law enforcement, the military, racing, sports, etc.)
Rating (0- 10) -	Rating (0- 10) -
(0 = not necessary for survival; 10 = necessary to save my life)	

Success scale-

How important is it to my success in life for me to...	
Continue harmful activities that are exciting? (e.g., excessive partying, risky sex or thrill crimes, etc.)	Develop exciting activities that are not harmful? (e.g., enter an exciting career in law enforcement, the military, racing, sports, etc.)
Rating (0- 10) -	Rating (0- 10) -
(0= not important at all; 10= so important I will never succeed in life without it)	

Severity scale-

How severe could the consequences be if I...	
Continue harmful activities that are exciting? (e.g., excessive partying, risky sex or thrill crimes, etc.)	Develop exciting activities that are not harmful? (e.g., enter an exciting career in law enforcement, the military, racing, sports, etc.)
Rating (0- 10) -	Rating (0- 10) -
(0= not severe at all; 10= very severe)	

Use the reality scale ratings above to "think though" the situation and write your responsible decision here- _____

Stopping Emotional Rumination on Avoidance of Pain (Relief Seeking)

Relief seeking by comforting yourself with harmful behavior is also a poor solution. Not only is using harmful behavior for relief seeking a poor solution because you have to pay in both cash and consequences, it is also a poor solution because it is temporarily and will wear off. The problem here is simple. First, there can be no comfort relief seeking (e.g., eating, drinking, drugging, smoking, spending, sex, etc.) without discomfort (e.g., depression, anxiety, anger). Second, as soon as the comfort relief seeking effects are over, the discomfort returns. Since this sets the occasion for doing the harmful behavior relapse again to relieve the discomfort, "Relapse is not the problem; it's a poor solution to the problem". If you don't think you are relief seeking to distract yourself from dealing with unwanted feelings or serious life problems and feel, "I do it because I like it and people I like do it", chances are that you have a low tolerance for rejection and a strong need for acceptance or attention. If this is the case you need to learn the ABC's of holding on to unwanted feelings to keep from acting them out through harmful behavior. A history of rejection by parents, partners or peers, puts you at risk for compromising yourself for acceptance or attention by doing things with others to fit in or feel accepted (e.g., unhealthy eating, drinking, drugging, sexual behavior). In the case of drugs and alcohol, you get pushed towards the behavior by direct avoidance of pain with emotion numbing chemical comfort at the same time you get pulled towards it by social acceptance from others who are also doing it.

If your avoidance of pain problem is fueled by an exaggerated need for acceptance or actual mental health symptoms (e.g., depression, anxiety, anger) self-medicating social discomfort, low-self esteem, feelings of inadequacy, depression, anxiety or anger is poor solution because it is temporarily. You need to solve the problem by getting directly at the cause of the pain beginning by using the ABC's of holding on to feelings to prevent avoiding the pain through harmful behavior. Think about it, unless you stop avoiding the pain (i.e., by eating, drinking, drugging, slugging, spending, sex, etc.), you will never be able to face it long enough to get used to it and channel it in the right direction. Complete the exercise below to show how you can use the ABC's of holding on to feelings in a situation that triggers a relief seeking relapse urge.

Accept the distressing feeling (Don't avoid or deny it, find a safe, quiet place, sit down, slow down and let yourself feel). Imagine that your need for acceptance gets triggered by depressing rejection, you have the opportunity to do a harmful behavior and you start ruminating on the relief you will get from that behavior. Describe a situation where that could happen to you and use the instructions in parentheses above to write how to accept the feeling.

_____

_____

Begin getting used to the feeling (Remind yourself that "Feelings can't hurt you, telling yourself "I can't stand it" hurts you." Think of a hot tub, don't get out, just sit with the sensation and let yourself get used to it). How could you begin to get used to the feeling?

_____

_____

Channel the feeling to the right place at the right time. (Give yourself time, delay action, remind yourself, "I can always [act on my feelings] tomorrow", then let go of all thinking and continue to sit with your sensations. Notice your nostrils as you breathe in and out. Feel your feet on the floor,. Stay in the moment and allow thoughtless peace right now. Think of the Chinese finger trap, stop struggling and just let it be so you can get free. When you're free take it to the right place.) Describe how to continue to sit with your sensations until you accommodate to your feelings and where you would take that problem after you are free from the emotional upset.

_____

_____

_____

Emotional Rumination Requires Positive Behavior Activation
The Social Problem Solving step of Taking responsible action, is based on a procedure called "Behavioral Activation" adapted to treat harmful behavior through "positive behavior activation". Positive behavior activation involves putting opposite extreme positive behaviors into action as competing responses to negative relapse thoughts, cravings and urges.

You can't just will unwanted thoughts and feelings out of your awareness. In order to get them off your mind, you have to stay busy and "Keep your problem up front", make your recovery your priority, go to the opposite extreme and set yourself up for success by planning a highly "structured day" of back to back healthy, helpful activities that prevents isolation, loneliness and boredom to support recovery and avoid relapse being triggered by unwanted feelings. Planning a structured day means becoming "the master of 15 minutes" and not allowing enough downtime to bring you down. "When the going gets tough, the tough get going" and protect their recovery with a structured day of positive activities.

If you are like most humans, you prefer being accepted over being rejected and prefer positive attention over being ignored. Since not getting acceptance and positive attention can result in relapse, it is important to get moving on developing a positive support network to meet human needs in a positive way. Support groups for your particular type of harmful behavior (i.e., eating, drinking, drugging, slugging, spending, sex, etc.) are the best place to start. However, at the same time, you need to develop an all consuming genuine, true interest or life goal. Beginning to associate with others who share the same positive interests or life goal helps you "keep your eyes on the prize" and not drift back into high risk situations for relapse. Planning a structured day around a genuine positive interest of life goal doesn't guarantee you will always be happy but it pretty much guarantees you won't be bored.

Combined Contributors to taking a Fall (relapse)
Combined emotional rumination and failure to consider consequences is a recipe for relapse. Taking a fall is likely from any of the following combinations of these high risk situations...
- Failure to consequences to others + emotional rumination on the pleasure you will get
- Failure to consequences to others + emotional rumination on the relief you will get
- Failure to consequences to self + emotional rumination on the pleasure you will get
- Failure to consequences to self + emotional rumination on the relief you will get
A summary of combined contributors to taking a fall is provided in Table 19 below.

Table 19
Combined Contributors to taking a Fall (relapse): Selected Examples

Ruminating on...	and Failure to Consider	Results in
Emotional upset and comfort food	Weight gain, body image depression	Unhealthy eating
Attention- from the opposite sex	Divorce	Trust abuse (cheating)
Acceptance- from using friends Excitement- getting high, good times, partying	failed urinalysis, probation violation, jail vehicular homicide	Substance abuse
Excitement- from thrill crime or envy of material things,	Arrest; jail	Property abuse (shoplifting)
Anger, revenge	Trauma to others; jail	Physical abuse
Excitement- from sex	Trauma to others; jail	Sexual abuse

Breaking the Stress-Relapse Cycle Summary
In summary, when Negative Coping (Phase 1) is used to avoid responsibility after making a mistake, Cover-up tactics (Phase 2) are then needed to avoid detection. Stress Buildup (Phase 3) from self-disappointment over making the mistake in the first place, the tension involved in covering it up or worry about being caught often wears the individual down to the point where they Slip or lapse (Phase 4) often by entering a high risk situation for relapse. Failure to escape from their high risk people, places or things eventually results in a Fall or relapse (Phase 5) back into unhealthy, harmful behavior. Remaining in a high risk situation until a self-control fall back into harmful behavior occurs may be motivated by: 1) approach of a reinforcing, pleasurable

state attached to the harmful behavior; or 2) avoidance/escape from current problems, unwanted feelings or unwanted thoughts (See Figure 4).

Awareness training needs to focus on how Recovery Perfectionism results in a self-control fall. Accept that recovery is two steps up, one back two up, etc. Realize that "a slip doesn't become a fall until you refuse to correct it" and learn to take immediate positive corrective action, like Olympic ice skaters who immediately correct a slip to avoid a fall. Responsibility training needs to focus on keeping consequences up front by continually doing a "Reality" check on what you are considering and practicing going to the opposite extreme [4] of unhealthy, harmful behavior fall with healthy, helpful behavior. Tolerance training requires learning to tolerate unwanted feelings, cravings and urges long enough to vent them in right place at the right time for the right reason. This involves knowing when to hold on to feelings, when to let them go and how to do it (i.e., with the ABC's of holding on and letting go of feelings). Challenging irresponsible thinking if very important to avoiding a fall.. For example, How awful would it be of you didn't respond? If you were duct taped to a chair and couldn't respond would you live through it? Why must it be done right now? Is there a state law that says you can't act on the feeling, urge or craving tomorrow? A summary description of going to the opposite extreme to recover from harmful behavior and prevent taking a fall back into harmful behavior is presented in Table 20.

Table 20.
Going to the Opposite to Recovery from Harmful Behavior

Fall (Relapse) A Responsibility Problem (giving up on self-control)	Recover (Go to the opposite extreme) Get back on track right away
Relapse into harmful, behavior through...	Avoid high risk situations or escape from them by...
Recovery Perfectionism	Challenging the irresponsible all or nothing thinking in perfectionism. "Slipping and taking a fall isn't as important as how fast you get up"- Think about Olympic skaters and block the skip give up trigger by correcting a slip as you are beginning to fall.
Failure to consider consequences to self or others	Using Fantasy Fast Forward and fast forward to the end to consider consequences. Consider the consequences of what you are considering, do a Reality Check. Think it through with the reality scales.
Emotional Rumination in unwanted trigger feelings (e.g., anxiety, depression, anger) or trigger thoughts (e.g., desire or revenge)	Being aware of magnifying, "Don't let it grow, let it go". Calm down using the ABC's of letting feelings go or get used to the feeling with the ABC's of holding on to feelings.

Five Relapse Cycle Questions need to be answered and addressed with ACTS healthy behavior success skills to help break your Stress-Relapse Cycle.

1. After making a mistake and falling back into your harmful behavior, what did you tell yourself to deal with it? (List one ACTS skill that you can use to stop Negative Coping.

_____

2. What did you do to keep your harmful behavior from being detected? (List one ACTS skill that you can use to stop a Cover Up.

_____

3. What stressful thoughts, feelings and situations are you experiencing? (List one ACTS skill that you can use to relieve Stress buildup

_____

4. What slips have you noticed that can lead you to fall back into your harmful behavior? (List one ACTS skill that you can use to correct a Slip

_____

5. What do you believe led you to fall back into your harmful behavior this last time? (List one ACTS skill that you can use to break a Fall

_____

Stress-Relapse Cycle Conclusion

Remember that stress is cumulative, it adds up until the threshold of acting out is reached and a relapse occurs. The Stress-Relapse Cycle helps you understand how negative coping, covering up problems, stress buildup and slips in awareness, judgment or self-control add up to trigger a fall back into harmful behavior. Each repetition of the Stress-Relapse Cycle increases problems with honesty, trust, loyalty, concern and responsibility (i.e., social maturity). Specifically, each time you fall back into your cycle: negative coping requires you to avoid *honesty* with yourself; cover up creates *trust* problems with others; stress buildup from not being loyal to what you know is right shifts your *loyalty* away from positive people who might confront you; careless slips reflect not showing enough *concern* for your recovery and; a fall back into harmful behavior is a self-control *responsibility* problem.

Typically we keep our Stress-Relapse Cycle going by staying in high risk situations, working ourselves up, not considering consequences and not solving problems. We do the same think over and over again assuming that next time we will have the willpower to avoid relapse. We need to finally accept that planning power beats willpower and start planning to Avoid trouble, Calm down, Think it through and Solve the problem.

> "Insanity: doing the same thing over and over again and expecting different results."
> -- Albert Einstein (1879- 1955)

Get honest about your Falls (relapses). Write a brief summary of the harmful life impact that you recorded above in the margins around the Stress Abuse Cycle on the worksheet at the end of this section that includes what you can do about it now (page 101). Discuss the impact that your harmful behavior has had on yourself and others with your therapist or treatment group. Log the date you discussed how you would typically Fall back into harmful behavior along with how to Recover (see Exhibit 2, p. 105) in the space provided below.

Date: _____ Discussed with: _____

Congratulations! You have now completed your work on understanding "The Stress-Relapse Cycle" that maintained, kept up or continued your unhealthy, harmful behavior. Make a presentation to your treatment group or therapist on how you developed your harmful behavior.

Complete your second of three self-evaluations using the form provided in Appendix E. If you are in treatment, discuss your self-evaluation with your therapist or group.

Workspace (Label your work) "Accept responsibility for your life. Know that it is you who will get you where you want to go, no one else."-- Les Brown (b. 1945)

_____

_____

_____

_____

_____

_____

_____

_____

_____

_____

_____

_____

_____

_____

_____

_____

_____

_____

_____

_____

_____

_____

_____

_____

_____

_____

_____

_____

_____

_____

_____

Workspace (Label your work)

"We must use time creatively and realize the time is always ripe to do right"-- Martin Luther King, Jr.

The Stress-Relapse Cycle Worksheet
How Harmful Behavior was Maintained

Name: _____

Date: _____

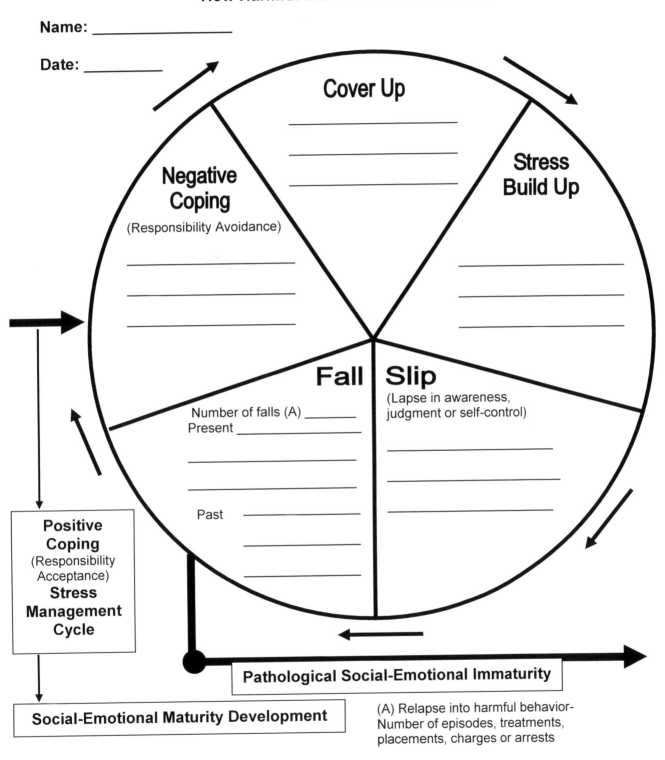

Cover Up

_____
_____
_____

Negative Coping
(Responsibility Avoidance)

_____
_____
_____

Stress Build Up

_____
_____

Fall

Number of falls (A) _____
Present _____

_____
_____

Past _____

_____
_____

Slip
(Lapse in awareness, judgment or self-control)

_____
_____
_____

Positive Coping
(Responsibility Acceptance)
Stress Management Cycle

Pathological Social-Emotional Immaturity

Social-Emotional Maturity Development

(A) Relapse into harmful behavior-
Number of episodes, treatments, placements, charges or arrests

Stress-Relapse Cycle Worksheet (continued)

Negative Coping (continued): _____
_____
_____
_____
_____
_____

Cover Up (continued): _____
_____
_____
_____

Stress Build-Up (continued): _____
_____
_____
_____

Slip (continued): _____
_____
_____
_____
_____

Fall (continued): Present Fall#1 (referral problem)-_____

Present Fall #2 (co-occurring harmful behavior with referral problem)- _____

Present Fall #3 (co-occurring harmful behavior with referral problem)- _____

Past Fall #1 (type of harmful behavior)- _____

Past Fall #2 (type of harmful behavior)- _____

Past Fall #3 (type of harmful behavior)- _____

Footnotes

1. "If you're not working on the solution, you're part of the problem" was adapted by Research Engineer Charles Russell Yokley for practical problems from 1968 San Francisco speech by Eldridge Cleaver (1935- present, American Black Leader, Writer), "What we're saying today is that you're either part of the solution or you're part of the problem".
2. "Act as if" by behaving like the person we should be than the person we have been is a key therapeutic community training method for positive change towards " right living" (Chapter 5, DeLeon, 2000) dating back to the early therapeutic community development period in the United States (1958- 1971).
3. "Right living" is a therapeutic community healthy positive lifestyle goal described in Chapter 5 of DeLeon, 2000 dating back to the early therapeutic community development period in the United States (1958- 1971).
4. Practicing going to the opposite extreme of negative attitudes and irresponsible behaviors by modeling positive attitudes and responsible behaviors is a key therapeutic community training method for positive change towards " right living" (Chapter 5, DeLeon, 2000) dating back to the early therapeutic community development period in the United States (1958- 1971). "You have to go to the opposite extreme [in treatment through the primary values of right living] to meet the median [after treatment]" is a time honored therapeutic community recovery maxim from Second Genesis founded in 1970 (program evaluated by Nemes, Wish and Messina, 1999).
5. A Singapore graduate student saying that reflects both Henry David Thoreau, "In the long run men hit only what they aim at. Therefore, though they should fail immediately, they had better aim at something high" (1817- 1862) and W. Clement Stone (1902- 2002), "Aim for the moon. If you miss, you may hit a star".
6. The healthy behavior success skills utilized were drawn from the following four research-supported intervention areas: Relapse Prevention; Emotional Regulation; Decisional Balance and; Social Problem Solving.
7. Rational Emotive Behavior Therapy (REBT) was developed by Dr. Albert Ellis. See Ellis & Bernard (2006) for further description of the REBT approach with children and Ellis & Velten (1992) for further description of REBT with adults exhibiting harmful, addictive behavior.
8. Adapted from "Knowledge is of two kinds. We know a subject ourselves, or we know where we can find information upon it." - Samuel Johnson (1709- 1784).
9. For case examples, see "the ART of Social Responsibility Therapy" (Ch. 2 in Yokley, 2008)

References

Ellis, A., & Bernard, M. E. (Eds.). (2006). *Rational emotive behavioral approaches to childhood disorders: Theory, practice and research*. New York, NY: Springer Science & Business Media Inc.

Ellis, A., & Velten, E. (1992). *When AA doesn't work for you: Rational steps to quitting alcohol*. Fort Lee, New Jersey: Barricade Books, Inc.

Yokley, J. (2011). Emotional Restitution Training in Social Responsibility Therapy for Sex Offender Referrals. In B. Schwartz (Ed.), Handbook of Sex Offender Treatment (Chapter 56). Kingston, NJ: Civic Research Institute. ISBN: 978-1-887554-03-9.

Yokley, J. (2010). How did I get this problem? Social Responsibility Therapy: Understanding Harmful Behavior Workbook 1. Cincinnati, OH: Social Solutions Press. ISBN: 978-0-9832449-0-5.

Yokley, J. (2008). *Social Responsibility Therapy for Adolescents and Young Adults: A Multicultural Treatment Manual for Harmful Behavior*, New York, NY, US: Routledge/Taylor and Francis Group. ISBN: 978-0-7890-3121-1.

Yokley, J. (2016). *The Clinician's Guide to Social Responsibility Therapy: Practical Applications, Theory and Research Support*. North Myrtle Beach, SC: Social Solutions Press.

Yokley, J. & Dudich, J. (in press). *Social Responsibility Therapy for Preteen Children: A Multicultural Treatment Manual for Harmful Behavior*. Bloomington, Indiana: Trafford Publishing.

Exhibit 1.
Managing Risk Factors for How Harmful Behavior was Acquired:
The Risk Factor Chain (that led to unhealthy, harmful behavior, i.e., biopsychosocial risk factors)
(Summary of risk factor coping skills in Workbook 1)

Note: A more complete set of "Treatment Notes" with case examples for each one of these categories is provided in "Understanding Harmful Behavior: A Social Responsibility Therapy Perspective." www.srtonline.org.

5. Initial Harmful Behavior (from interaction of all risk factors resulting in underdeveloped social-emotional maturity) Realize how focusing on the past and others behavior, problems with social-emotional maturity, not avoiding or escaping high risk situations and using irresponsible thinking led to behavior that was harmful to self and/or others.

4. Cognitive Risk Factors (Irresponsible Thinking) Continuously be on the lookout for irresponsible self-statements that cause problems, e.g., Justifying actions based on feelings, taking the victim view, blaming others and using the words "just" or "only" to minimize errors in order to avoid having to correct them.

3. Situational Risk Factors (High Risk Situations) Develop high risk situation escape and avoidance plans before you leave the house. "If you fail to plan, you plan to fail" and every morning set a daily relapse prevention & responsibility achievement plan ("Today I will escape…, avoid… and maintain…")

Not your responsibility then

2. Social-Emotional Risk Factors (Social & emotional maturity problems) Realize that confidence is built by a strong sense of identity and that who you are is what you stand for, not what you look like, who you know or what you have. Know that "If you don't stand for something you'll fall for anything". Decide to stand for honesty, trust, loyalty, concern and responsibility.

Note: <u>Social maturity</u>= honesty, trust, loyalty, concern & responsibility; <u>Emotional maturity</u>= self-awareness, self-efficacy & self-control.

1. Historical Risk Factors (Past traumatic events or things that created permanent problems) Remember- There are only two things that you can't change in life, the past and other people's behavior and one guaranteed way to make yourself feel helpless is by continually focusing on either. Empower yourself by looking at what you can change (the present and your behavior) not things you can't change which lead to feeling helpless. Use the ABC's of letting go of feelings (see Positive Coping, p. 9)

Your responsibility now

Note: Includes biopsychosocial disadvantages, physical, social, emotional trauma history & other predisposing factors

Exhibit 2.
Recovery Behavior Maintenance: The Stress Management Cycle (that maintains appropriate social behavior control and develops social-emotional maturity)
(Summary of stress management skills in Workbook 2)

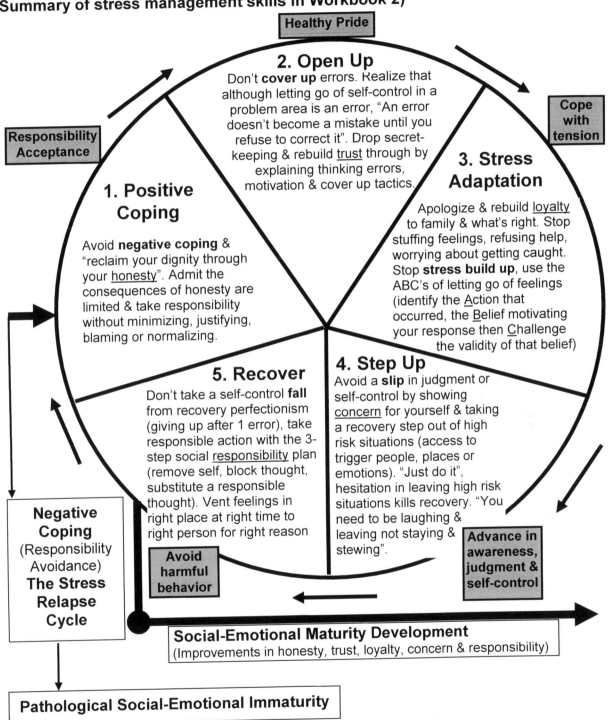

Healthy Pride

2. Open Up
Don't **cover up** errors. Realize that although letting go of self-control in a problem area is an error, "An error doesn't become a mistake until you refuse to correct it". Drop secret-keeping & rebuild <u>trust</u> through by explaining thinking errors, motivation & cover up tactics.

Responsibility Acceptance

Cope with tension

1. Positive Coping
Avoid **negative coping** & "reclaim your dignity through your <u>honesty</u>". Admit the consequences of honesty are limited & take responsibility without minimizing, justifying, blaming or normalizing.

3. Stress Adaptation
Apologize & rebuild <u>loyalty</u> to family & what's right. Stop stuffing feelings, refusing help, worrying about getting caught. Stop **stress build up**, use the ABC's of letting go of feelings (identify the <u>A</u>ction that occurred, the <u>B</u>elief motivating your response then <u>C</u>hallenge the validity of that belief)

5. Recover
Don't take a self-control **fall** from recovery perfectionism (giving up after 1 error), take responsible action with the 3-step social <u>responsibility</u> plan (remove self, block thought, substitute a responsible thought). Vent feelings in right place at right time to right person for right reason

4. Step Up
Avoid a **slip** in judgment or self-control by showing <u>concern</u> for yourself & taking a recovery step out of high risk situations (access to trigger people, places or emotions). "Just do it", hesitation in leaving high risk situations kills recovery. "You need to be laughing & leaving not staying & stewing".

Avoid harmful behavior

Advance in awareness, judgment & self-control

Negative Coping (Responsibility Avoidance) **The Stress Relapse Cycle**

Social-Emotional Maturity Development
(Improvements in honesty, trust, loyalty, concern & responsibility)

Pathological Social-Emotional Immaturity

Exhibit 3. Addressing Factors that Support Multiple forms of Harmful Behavior[1] (Summary of prosocial behavior skills in Workbook 3)

How Harmful Behavior was Generalized: The Harmful Behavior Anatomy

(of the pathological social-emotional immaturity that supports harmful behavior)

Get honest with yourself about all forms of harmful behavior:
Sexual abuse- including promiscuity
Physical abuse- including threats
Property abuse- theft, vandalism, gambling, spending
Substance abuse- drugs, alcohol, smoking, overeating
Trust abuse- lying, cheating, misleading

Challenge irresponsible thinking using 10 point reality scales. Survival Scale- how necessary for actual survival it is to do the behavior being considered 0= not necessary at all, 10= absolutely necessary to save my life right now. Success Scale- how important for success doing the responsible thing or failing to do it would be 0= not important at all, 10= so important that it could change my entire life). Severity Scale- how severe doing the responsible thing or failing to do it would be 0= not severe at all: 10= so severe that my head could explode.

Using the ABC's of letting pride go (of fear of looking bad, rejection, reticule) is important in learning to accept feedback, admit mistakes, avoid denial and cover up.

Irresponsible Thinking Avoid unhealthy recovery perfectionism (giving up after a single error) & develop healthy perfectionism by accepting that "doing right is more important than being right" & mobilizing tenacity by realizing "When the going gets tough the tough get going" & finishing your responsibilities.

"The truth will set you free"- Be honest with others about your behavior and honest with yourself about your feelings. Admit that feelings can't hurt you or your self-control but telling yourself that you can't stand the feelings causes actions that hurt you.

Admit that you want honesty, trust, loyalty, concern and responsibility from others and start working hard on giving it in order to get it.

Unhealthy Pride

Control And Power Obsession

Deception

Social Maturity Deficit

Emotional Maturity Deficit

Unhealthy Perfectionism

Let go of "I can handle it", admit that the key to relapse is access & escape or avoid high risk situations.

Grandiosity

Develop: self-awareness though feedback "Other people see you better than you see yourself"; self-efficacy through evening responsibility review of 3 things that went right & how you made it happen; self-control through ABC's of holding on to feelings (Accept the feeling, Begin getting used to it & Channel it to the right place at the right time.

Maladaptive Self-image

"Image isn't everything, responsibility is". Become aware of the image you project around others and your reasons. Then put your effort into trying to be socially responsible by realizing that you don't have to be #1, famous, gorgeous, rich or feared to survive or succeed in life.

CAPO

Realize that real power comes from self-control, not control of others or moods through over eating, drinking, fighting, sexualizing or spending. Ask yourself "Why should I hurt me just because other people or other things hurt me" and stop hurting yourself by acting on feelings

Self-defeating Habits

Look at your social needs & evaluate whether your need for acceptance, attention or excitement is causing you to compromise yourself, be unassertive, exaggerate or take unnecessary risks. Stop score keeping & getting even & "Be all you can be" by realizing that "The best revenge is success"

Appendix A.
Information for Mental Health Professionals

Case examples and intervention descriptions in this workbook are provided in "Social Responsibility Therapy for Adolescents & Young Adults: A Multicultural Treatment Manual for Harmful Behavior" (see p. 141). Clinician instructions on using this workbook are provided in "The Clinician's Guide to Social Responsibility Therapy: Practical Applications, Theory and Research Support " (p. 143). Originally developed for client use with therapist input to help those in treatment become more active participants, this workbook provides the high level of structure needed for clients in institutions or residential care where more self-directed workbook structured discovery is necessary. This structured discovery workbook can also provide self-awareness homework assignments for session discussion with outpatient clients in need of structure between sessions and relapse prevention support. The vocabulary bar has been set relatively high for self-help workbooks to encourage cognitive as well as social-emotional growth. This allows therapists to encourage clients whose unhealthy, harmful behavior has interfered with their education to improve their vocabulary by looking up definitions of words that they never learned and sharing them in sessions with therapist prompting. It also give the client practice asking for help on less emotionally charged issues.

Integrating stand alone components- If you look at Figure 1, you will see that there are three sections in The Problem Development Triad: the first has five structured discovery learning experience units on understanding of how harmful behavior was acquired; the second section also has five learning experience units on how harmful behavior was maintained and; the third section has 10 learning experience units on factors that allow harmful behavior to generalize or be substituted for other problem behavior making a total of 20 structured discovery units to cover. These three sections are covered in three "stand alone" workbooks that can be integrated into existing treatments individually. If you are seeking to reinforce the portion of your treatment that develops insight into how clients acquired their condition over time, you can implement workbook one. If you wish to reinforce the relapse prevention portion of your treatment by developing client understanding of how they maintained their problem behavior when others stopped, you can implement workbook two. You can implement workbook three if your client exhibits multiple forms of harmful behavior (i.e., co-occurring disorders) or if you wish to address concerns about their harmful behavior generalizing to other problem areas (e.g., behavior migration to another problem during treatment). However, a solid harmful behavior recovery understanding and emotional restitution through Problem Development Triad presentation on how their harmful behavior was acquired, maintained and generalized will require Structured Discovery learning during the completion of all three workbooks.

Group therapy- If you are running a treatment group or program where individuals start treatment at different times, the three workbooks can be completed in any order but require an introduction session before each which has an overview of the Problem Development Triad. As in individual/family therapy a summary of what has been learned is needed at the end of each section along with one presentation session per person in treatment. In group therapy sessions that are time limited (e.g., 1 ½ hours per session for 6- 8 members), it may not be possible to cover all issues for all clients so prioritize by making sure you cover the top three first. This can be done easily by asking each group member to list several section (i.e., link in workbook 1, phase in workbook 2 or component in workbook 3) descriptors that they rated highest and most important to their recovery. Hold one session for each section where the topic of discussion is the characteristics that were rated highest in that section. Reinforce the healthy relationship success skills (p. 18- 19) and teach the healthy behavior success skills (p.19- 27) as indicated. Create "instant identification" by pulling together similarities with a show of hands, e.g., "Who else rated this characteristic as a 2 or above?" discuss those common characteristics. Then move on to the next person asking for three that haven't been discussed. Usually after several people have talked in a group of 6- 8, the top symptom of that component has been covered for each group member and the group can be moved to processing how that problem affected their life and to generating one positive coping skill to use for each problem characteristic discussed with the homework assignment of using those coping skills on their Situation Response Analysis Logs (Appendix D, p. 127). Note: A simplified version may have to be implemented by the therapist for low functioning groups and examples are available from www.srtonline.org.

Social Responsibility Therapy Group Process Skills- Since unhealthy, harmful behavior is multicultural, the demographic makeup of Social Responsibility Therapy groups is diverse. Given this situation a set of SRT multicultural group unity development "PRAISE" skills was designed for motivational enhancement of client participation in the diverse group setting. The "PRAISE" acronym helps SRT therapists remember the social learning procedures used to facilitate groups by **P**ulling people into the group process, **R**esponsible reinforcement, **A**cknowledgement of contributions, **I**nstant identification, **S**ocial mathematics to discover common participant denominators and **E**nabling responsibility. These skills are pulled from Yokley (2008) on the page numbers listed in parentheses on these PRAISE cue card (p. 28) and are described further in The Clinician's Guide to SRT (see p. 143). These skills need to be modeled for clients by therapists during all discussions of SRT workbook issues and social-emotional maturity issues to develop multicultural group unity and therapeutic participation. All occasions of clients using these skills in group should be verbally reinforced by therapists.

Individual/family therapy- A set of SRT individual therapy problem "REPAIR" collaboration skills was designed for motivational enhancement in individual sessions from two person centered and four SRT participation motivation skills. The "REPAIR" acronym helps SRT therapists remember the following relationship collaboration skills: **R**eflection, **E**ncouraging, **P**ulling the client in, **A**cknowledgement, **I**dentification and **R**esponsible Reinforcement. If you are doing individual/family therapy with a focus on insight into how clients acquired their condition over time, you can complete workbook one in 5- 6 sessions. If you wish to focus individual therapy on relapse prevention of harmful behavior you can complete workbook two in 5- 6 sessions and if you focus is on co-occurring disorders, you can complete workbook 3 in 10- 12 sessions. Problem Development Triad presentations take between one and two hours per person depending on the extent of the harmful behavior history. Whether implemented individually or in group, all three workbooks can be completed in 24- 25 weekly outpatient sessions or an eight week intensive outpatient program with sessions Monday, Wednesday and Friday.

Abbreviated version- Social Responsibility Therapy can accommodate an abbreviated version for treatment session limitations that are sometimes imposed by program length or funding source session limitations. In all three workbooks, introduce the topic of each section (i.e., workbook 1 link, workbook 2 phase or workbook 3 component) and start with a writing assignment on "What I know about this topic". Then cover the top three key characteristics or concepts to cover and move on to the nest section topic. This allows covering more than one section in each treatment session. If you do Appendix D Candy Bar exercise, discuss the high risk access in all cases.

Repetition- Implement three repetitions of each section to reinforce learning. For example: 1) have client read and complete exercises in a section marking areas that need clarification; 2) review section with client, translating material, clarifying areas as needed and asking key concept questions; 3) have client teach the concepts learned and share personal information/discoveries with appropriate others. This is often done with: 1) a homework assignment; 2) an individual session and; 3) a group/family session.

Adjustment for special needs- Reading level can be ahead of math simply because reading is used more in the everyday life of many people. Thus is not uncommon to see clients do well in rating all of the characteristics in a section and transcribing their top three to their worksheet correctly but getting the math wrong and showing low average scores next to severe behavior statements with high statement ratings. If you have individuals like this, handle it the same way that you would doing the abbreviated version for time constraints by focusing your discussion on the top three rated characteristics in each component which does not require calculating each component average rating score. Special needs in secure residential or correctional settings may require therapists to sign off at the end of each section under the "Discussed with" heading in order to get required completion certificates.

Self-evaluations- Treatment programs addressing harmful behavior often have their participants review their self-evaluations at the end of each Problem Development Triad section in a group treatment setting with their peers and staff. Promotion to the next program phase or requests for increases in program privileges are typically linked to successful progress in social-emotional maturity development (i.e., honesty, trust, loyalty, concern, responsibility, self-awareness, self-efficacy and self-control). The same process can be used in family therapy meetings where teen privileges are based on social-emotional maturity progress.

Client reinforcement- Staff who have used this manual successfully in the past with the highest level of participation, provided client accomplishment awards (e.g., certificates of completion for adults which included tangible reinforcement for youth) after the completion of each section. Explaining how you fell back into harmful behavior in several Stress-Relapse Cycle presentations helps diffuse mandated treatment resentment.

Basic Awareness Training, Responsibility Training & Tolerance Training- During implementation of Social Responsibility Therapy, basic Awareness, Responsibility and Tolerance Training tools are needed to deal with the emotional baggage related to past historical trauma and self-disappointment from acquiring harmful behavior habits. Basic Awareness Training tools include the need to become aware of the Irresponsible Thinking (listed in Appendix C) that enables harmful behavior as well as responsible alternatives that need to be substituted. In addition, it is important to help clients develop an acute awareness of the basic high risk situations (i.e., people, places and emotions) that can trigger falling back into the *Stress-Relapse Cycle* and relapse. Basic Tolerance Training tools include an emotional regulation procedure to help clients let go of their emotions (p. 22- 23), dissipating them so that they do not contribute to the *Stress Build Up* that leads to a *Slip* and *Fall* back into harmful behavior relapse. Another emotional regulation procedure is needed to help clients hold on to their emotions (p. 23-24) long enough to accommodate to them and take them to the right place in order to avoid displacing feelings on others. Basic Responsibility Training tools include a relapse prevention procedure to help clients escape high risk situations (p. 19). A second important basic relapse prevention tool is needed to help clients with the ongoing responsible decision making that can set the relapse process in motion (p. 24- 25). Awareness Training on Irresponsible Thinking and High Risk Situations is prerequisite to the effective use of the healthy relationship and behavior success skills covered in this workbook (p. 18- 27). As indicated in the "Summary of Healthy Relationship and Behavior Success Skills" (p. 17), during Awareness Training in this workbook on how harmful behavior was acquired, basic Responsibility and Tolerance Training tools need to be used to address the problems that led to harmful behavior, maintained it and helped it spread to other areas. A summary of the basic interventions that need to be integrated into The Problem Development Triad is provided in Exhibits 1- 3 (p. 104- 106).

Appendix B.
Self-Awareness Problems & Relapse: Foresight Deficit Decisions
(also referred to as Apparently Irrelevant Decisions or Seemingly Unimportant Decisions)
"The road to hell is paved with good intentions" -- John Ray circa 1670

Nowhere is the importance of developing self-awareness and using foresight as clear as in the case of Foresight Deficit Decisions. Foresight Deficit Decisions are decisions made without enough foresight or thinking ahead and awareness of high risk situations. These decisions pave the road to harmful behavior relapse often beginning with good intentions. Relapse from Foresight Deficit Decisions often occurs from Problem priorities or Triage Trouble. Triage is French for "to sort" and refers to emergency room sorting of battle and disaster victims in a system of priorities designed to maximize the number of survivors. Problem priorities involves not keeping the focus on the most important problem first. In terms of harmful behavior relapse prevention, problem priorities involves getting diverted away from "keeping your problem up front". This often relates to good intentions, putting other people or tasks first, forgetting about self and letting priorities slip. This can occur from assuming that good intentions can be substituted for good foresight and planning.

In reality, no matter how good our intentions are, if we don't use positive planning, stick to our recovery priorities (i.e., relapse prevention plan), avoid high risk situations, use Fantasy Fast Forward (p. 113) and the reality scales (p. 24- 25) to think it through and weigh the possible consequences, Murphy's Law will take hold and "whatever can go wrong, will go wrong". Foresight deficit decisions or slips occur in virtually all forms of harmful behavior relapse. The following examples illustrate that the key to controlling harmful behavior is developing enough self-awareness to make relapse prevention decisions and avoid the foresight slips that lead there.

A trust abuse (cheating, overspending) example would be the foresight deficit decision by an individual having partner jealousy problems to stop in a flower shop where an ex-girlfriend worked for two dozen roses to smooth things over (slip #1, diversion away from "keeping your problem up front" by good intentions). The thought that seeing his ex-girlfriend might not be a good idea was immediately replaced by the self-statement, "this would be a good test of our relationship" (slip #2, testing self-control). In the shop, the ex-girlfriend commented about the expensive purchase stating "You must really care" which led to the honest answer that the flowers were to try and patch things up (slip #3, diplomacy lapse). This started a discussion of things that had gone wrong (slip #4, inappropriate self-disclosure) which led to talking about the good times they used to have together which led to being invited over to her place "just for a drink" (slip #5 minimizing). That conversation led to rekindling an old flame which resulted in spending the night and giving the roses to the ex-girlfriend the following morning on the way out the door. Feeling very guilty about cheating, they went online and booked an expensive weekend getaway trip to make it up to their partner which put them back into heavy credit card debt. Thus, the foresight deficit decision to buy roses at a shop where an ex-girlfriend worked in order to smooth over a partner conflict, triggered a chain of events which set the occasion for relapse on cheating and overspending.

A substance abuse (food) example would be the foresight deficit decision by an overweight individual in a diet program to turn down the cash alternative and accept a cruise that they won at the office work incentive program. This occurred as a result of telling themselves, "I know there's a lot of food on those cruises but wouldn't it be great to do something nice for the family?" (slip #1, careless exposure to a high risk situation with good intentions). The first night of the cruise, ballroom dancing was scheduled to follow a gourmet dinner. They ordered healthy food and ate reasonable portions but after dinner the dancing announcement included an invitation to a complete dessert buffet in the adjoining room for those who didn't want to dance. Their partner took their hand and led them into the dessert buffet as opposed to the dance floor as was expected (slip #2, failure to communicate needs and plan ahead). Not wanting to be a burden they went along (slip #3, compromising self to be accepted) telling themselves "I'll just tag along but will leave if it gets too much" (slip #4, testing self-control) which it quickly did and they left to sit down at one of the tables stating "you go ahead, I'm resting up for dancing". Their partner returned to the table with two plates, put one on front of them that was filled with all of their dessert favorites and stated "This is for your hard earned work that brought us here". They told themselves, "Why not, I deserve a reward" and joined in as opposed to speaking up for themselves (slip #5, rationalizing harmful behavior through feelings of entitlement). Thus, the foresight deficit decision to accept a cruise trip as opposed to taking the cash alternative triggered a chain of events which set the occasion for a diet relapse.

A substance abuse (cigarettes) example would be the foresight deficit decision by an individual who just quit smoking to go over and say hello to some friends they see sitting in the smoking section of a restaurant (slip #1, careless exposure to a high risk situation with good intentions). Having not seen them for some time, they accepted an invitation to sit down and visit because they felt a little awkward about eating alone anyway (slip #2, failure to implement a concrete face saving exit strategy and justifying actions based on feelings). After dinner their smoking friends all lit up and the smell filled the air reminding them of that great feeling that they used to get from a cigarette after a good meal (slip #3, dwelling on euphoric recall). They were caught off guard and were in a sort of daydream trance thinking about it when asked, "Want one?" with their favorite brand being dangled right under their nose. They remember thinking "Just one won't hurt" (slip #4, minimizing harmful behavior) as they took the lighter that was being passed to them. Thus, the foresight deficit decision to join some friends in the smoking section of a restaurant to catch up on old times triggered a chain of events which set the occasion for a smoking relapse.

A substance abuse (marijuana) example would be the foresight deficit decision by an individual in their first week of residential substance abuse treatment to call their partner without discussing it with staff to reassure them that everything will work out fine (slip #1, diversion away from "keeping your problem up front" by good intentions). This call triggered feeling emotionally threatened when their partner seemed to be getting along fine without them which led to a fear that the relationship would be lost if they stayed in treatment because their partner might find someone else (slip #2, affect impaired perception). Since the focus of their residential substance abuse treatment was on learning to deal with self and contact with outsiders is initially discouraged, this fear was not disclosed to others (slip #3, unhealthy pride) causing Stress Build-

Up which set the occasion for the belief that "I must go over there to make sure everything is OK or something will go wrong" (slip #4, irresponsible thinking and Control and Power Obsession). This led to calling a friend to pick them up and sneaking out during a community AA meeting (slip #5, deception). When they arrived at their partner's place, a party was going on where everyone was getting high but they do not leave (slip #6, failure to exit a high risk situation) because there are only five other people at the party and they assumed that the party was planned for three couples (slip #7, assuming thinking error). This assumption validated up their fear that they would lose their partner if they stayed in treatment at the same time that someone passed them a joint and they felt the need to smoke marijuana to calm themselves down (slip #8, justifying actions based on feelings). Thus, the foresight deficit decision to call their partner for reassurance triggered a chain of events which set the occasion for a marijuana abuse relapse.

A property abuse (gambling, credit card debt) example would be the foresight deficit decision by an individual in gamblers anonymous to take a weekend convenience store job in addition to their regular office job to pay off their considerable gambling debt and deciding to stay after learning they would be running the store by themselves (slip #1, careless exposure to a high risk situation with good intentions). The fact that lottery ticket sales were a large part of the business wasn't considered a problem because their gambling debt occurred at the horse races (slip #2, rationalizing, tunnel vision). The following weekend, a customer won $1,000 on an instant win scratch off ticket and gave him a $20 tip. He told himself that he wasn't gambling because it wasn't his money (slip #3, self-deception), he put the $20 in the register and scratched off $20 worth of instant win tickets. Telling himself that one more wouldn't hurt (slip #5, pushing back the line), he scratched off another one and when it didn't hit, got mad and told himself, "Why pay for something that isn't worth anything?" (slip #4, justifying actions based on feelings). By the end of his shift he had scratched off $50 worth of instant win tickets and didn't have the cash to pay for them. He had to leave the store unattended to go across the street and use the bank machine putting himself further into credit card debt to avoid being charged with stealing on the job. Thus, the foresight deficit decision to stay in a weekend convenience store job that allowed unsupervised access to lottery tickets in order to pay off a gambling debt, triggered a chain of events which set the occasion for a gambling and credit card debt relapse.

A property abuse (theft) example would be the foresight deficit decision by an individual who was just fined for shoplifting to borrow a nice leather coat for a social occasion from a friend at the last minute (slip #1, not keeping their problem "up front"). Finding the friend absent triggered frustration and borrowing the coat without asking or leaving a note because of being late (slip #2, justifying actions based on feelings). Not waiting to find the person or taking the time to write a note (slip #3, feeding the Problem of Immediate Gratification) set the occasion for telling self, "I might as well keep the coat because I already have it and nobody knows" (slip #4, rationalizing). Thus, the foresight deficit decision to borrow a coat for a social occasion from an absent friend triggered a series of events which set the occasion for a stealing relapse.

A physical abuse (domestic violence) example would be the foresight deficit decision by an individual who was warned by their probation officer to stay away from their ex-partner to drop in and apologize for the way they acted (slip #1, "my way" attitude). Upon arriving at the house they noticed there was a strange car in the driveway which triggered immediate suspicion and jealousy (slip #2, affect impaired perception). Telling themselves, "I have to know", they barged in the house without knocking (slip #3, Control and Power Obsession) only to find their partner hugging someone else. Without thinking, they yelled out "Who are you?" only to hear the same thing back which instantly confirmed their worst fears (slip #4, assuming) and triggered an attack on what later was found to be a cousin in town for a family funeral. Thus, the foresight deficit decision to drop in and apologize to ex-partner for their behavior triggered a series of events which set the occasion for a domestic violence relapse.

A sexual abuse (adult and adolescent) example would be the foresight deficit decision for an adult in sex offender treatment to put off their regular lunch time trip to the dry cleaners at the mall on Friday (when the number of potential victims to stare at is minimal) to take a friend having problems out to lunch (adult slip #1, problem priorities) or for an adolescent in sex offender treatment to accept a babysitting job because they were pressured to do it (adolescent slip #1, problem priorities). The adult became overwhelmed with a sexual urge from being exposed to several attractive potential victims as they walked through the mall on Saturday with their dry cleaning and the adolescent became overwhelmed with a sexual urge after they walked through the door to greet the children on their babysitting job saw their potential victims and heard the parents tell the children, "Now you do everything your babysitter tells you" (slip #2, failure to plan ahead). In both cases, they maintained visual contact which triggered a flood of mental "snap shots" (slip #3, failure to exit a high risk situation) telling themselves they were "just" staring to get a mental picture for masturbation later in private and had no intent to touch the person (slip #4, pushing back the line). The result was that the adult found themselves automatically following someone out into the parking lot and the adolescent found themselves deciding to give one of the children a bath. Thus, the foresight deficit decision of the adult to postpone a regular dry cleaning trip in order to help a friend out or the adolescent to accepting a babysitting job to help an adult out started a chain of events which set the occasion for a sexual abuse relapse.

Fantasy Fast Forward

Foresight Deficit Decisions can be avoided by using "Fantasy Fast Forward". Fantasy Fast Forward involves viewing the situation you are considering (often a favor or something that involves good intentions) like a movie with you as the main character. Run it through your mind and fast forward to think ahead. Play the movie through to the end in your mind, stop at each decision step and ask yourself "In the worst case what could happen if I take this step?" Use a Reality Check (p. 13) to consider the consequences and determine whether to go ahead or tell yourself "I'm not falling into that" and change your course.

Appendix C.
Types of Irresponsible Thinking & Responsible Alternatives

Responsible Self-statement Substitution is identifying and correcting the irresponsible thinking that gets in the way of you getting what you want in life. This basically involves learning to talk to yourself like someone who really cares about you. If you were standing next to your most responsible best friend in the whole world in a high risk situation for relapse, they would encourage you to do the right thing and steer you towards a responsible behavior. Talking to yourself like your own best friend involves asking yourself "what would someone who really cares about me, tell me to do?" Although most of us know our best friends really well, since we can't actually read minds, one easy way to talk to yourself like your own best friend, steer yourself away from irresponsible, harmful, negative behavior and towards a responsible, helpful, positive alternative is to use the Pendulum Concept (p. 14), "go to the opposite extreme" and do the responsible, helpful opposite. Harmful thinking and helpful opposites are listed below.

1. Deception- Examples include… Outright <u>Lying</u> (not being truthful to others) or covering up and avoiding admitting responsibility along with <u>Denial</u> (not being truthful to self), e.g., "It's not my fault", "It just happened", <u>Diversion</u> (changing the subject, disclosing a minor problem to avoid discussion of a major one, shifting the focus to unnecessary facts, details, other problems or people, "They started it") & <u>Division</u> (misleading & splitting people against each other, often into camps that defend or challenge your innocence, "I really didn't do anything wrong"). <u>Vagueness</u>, <u>Dishonesty by omission</u> & <u>Legitimizing</u> (leaving out critical information or misleading with partial information to avoid consequences), A lack of understanding about the difference between dishonesty by omission (withholding information for selfish reasons) and diplomacy (withholding information for unselfish reasons) can also cause problems. <u>Appeasing</u> (telling people what they want to hear), <u>Assenting</u> (agreeing without meaning it and having no intention to comply). Bending the truth to meet needs for attention (e.g., exaggerating a story for entertainment, bragging), acceptance (e.g., gossiping to fit in, giving insincere complements) or excitement (e.g., saying whatever it takes to get someone to have sex) can result in harm to both self and others. Deception which involves basic honesty deficits (not enough) is only one side of the coin. Honesty problems can also involve excesses (too much). Angry over-disclosure of truthful and painful details (brutal honesty) that hurt another's feelings is the most common example. In addition, inappropriate self-disclosure (excessive honesty) for the situation due to social anxiety (nervous talking) can end up hurting you. Disclosing confidential information when asked about someone else (excessive honesty) can result in harm to others. Whether the honesty issues involve a deficit or excess, the results are still harmful to self or others.

Helpful opposite- Get Honest. "Honesty is the best policy" (Miguel de Cervantes, 1547-1616). Admit that the reason honesty is valued so much is the tremendous price attached. Help yourself get honest by realizing that getting honest and taking responsibility is having the courage to face consequences and take pride in your courage to get honest. Use the ABC's of letting feelings go to "Calm down" (see p. 22) so that you don't justify your actions (lying) based on your feelings (fear of consequences). Before you use deception, "Think it through" using the reality scales (p. 24) to weigh out the severity of the consequences to yourself and others. Get honest about your mistakes and the mistakes of others right away to help yourself and others avoid getting in worse trouble later. Tell yourself the truth about the feelings that others could have about your actions and how you feel about the actions of others.

Then avoid stress buildup that can trigger relapse by talking out mistakes and feelings with a therapist or someone who is responsible.

2. Double standards- Examples include… No concept of social exchange where there is an expectation that good deeds are returned & favors are repaid. Everything is one sided. "Do as I say, not as I do". <u>Honesty double standards,</u> not being completely honest and refusing to admit responsibility while telling yourself others "should" level with you. Being more honest with others about their behavior than you are with yourself about yours or being more honest with yourself than you are with others. <u>Trust double standards-</u> Believes they are trustworthy but distrusts others. Has "Trust Entitlement", feels entitled to be trusted (and receive associated privileges based on "innocent until proven guilty" rationalization) despite lack of responsibility but unwilling to trust others. Doesn't understand that trust must be earned by consistent honesty and responsible action. <u>Loyalty double standards</u> involve shifting loyalties and cheating but expecting or demanding loyalty from others. <u>Concern double standards,</u> taking more than you give, being selfish while complaining about, expecting or demanding concern from others. Being a selfish friend or life partner by looking for support and affection without looking for the opportunity to provide it. <u>Responsibility double standards,</u> being irresponsible while complaining about, expecting or demanding responsibility from others. <u>Respect double standards-</u> being disrespectful while complaining about, expecting or demanding respect from others. This can relate to a 2:1 input/output multiplication/division problem occurs when feedback from others is viewed as twice as critical as it was & statements to others are viewed as half as critical as they were. This is because of hypersensitivity to what comes in (magnifying it, multiplying by 2), expecting it to be criticism, aversive or disrespectful in nature (e.g., Viewing "I don't think I agree" as "You turned on me" or "You stupid ass…") & being insensitive to what is let out in terms of criticism, aversive or disrespectful comments (minimizing it, dividing by 2) often due to a role reversal deficit and not putting self in other peoples shoes, e.g., Stating "You back stabbing ass…." or "You dumb ass…" as opposed to "This is important to me so I'd like to know why you don't agree". Viewing disagreement as disrespect and using fear or manipulation to get agreement. In summary, either showing more respect and consideration for yourself than you do for others or showing more respect and consideration for others than you do for yourself. <u>Behavioral double standards-</u> Mistakes you make are considered accidents but mistakes others make are assumed to be on purpose. In parenting, "Do what I say, not what I do".

Helpful opposite- Treat others the way you want to be treated. Use your healthy relationship success skills (p. 18) and practice social exchange by returning favors, compliments, respect and social responsibility (i.e., honesty, trust, loyalty, concern and responsibility). Hold yourself to the same standards that you expect from others. Realize that others are likely to give you the same thing that you give to them. This means being aware of the fact that humans can easily fall into double standards and avoiding double standards in honesty, trust, loyalty, concern and responsibility. Letting go of double standards means having the courage to correct yourself after a mistake in honesty, trust, loyalty, concern or responsibility. Use the reality scales to help you "Think it through" (p. 24) and realize that you can handle correcting yourself after a mistake.

While all double standards are important to work on, trust double standards is particularly important since many people feel that they can be trusted but do not trust others. While trust double standards may relate to years of exposure to television news covering the scandals if those who are not trustworthy, it is still an important issue because "Every kind of peaceful cooperation among men is primarily based on mutual trust and only secondarily on institutions such as courts of justice and police" (Albert Einstein, 1879-1955). Help yourself build trust in others by realizing that there is something in it for you. Realize that you get more privileges as a youth and promotions as an adult "after" you develop trust by being responsible. The key word here is "after". Trust is not a legal right, where you are innocent until proven guilty so don't tell yourself "they should trust me until I prove myself untrustworthy". Since you don't trust others that you don't know well, you can't expect others to trust you without first getting to know you. Just like others have to earn your trust, you have to earn theirs. The point that others are likely to give you the same thing you give them is easy to see with honesty. If you are dishonest with others, they are likely to be dishonest with you. This point can be a little confusing in terms of *building trust* unless you realize that responsibility is involved. If you are responsible with others (i.e., do what you say, when you say for the reason you say), they are likely to trust you and if others are responsible with you, you are likely to trust them. The same thing applies with *learning to trust* which can also be confusing unless you realize that honesty is involved. If you pick honest people to trust and open up with your honest feelings to them, they are likely to view you as an honest person and open up with their honest feelings to you. Picking an honest person to trust is the key here.

3. Irresponsible Loyalty- Examples include… Forming negative ties, developing relationships with irresponsible others. Being loyal to people you can't count on and who get you in trouble by telling you what you want to hear not what you need to hear or asking you to do something wrong. Unhealthy dependency on people who can't be depended on, continuing to give more than you get, overly loyal, remaining in relationships with others who are not dependable or shifting loyalty, problems with attachment and getting close and staying close. Holding Negative contracts, i.e., "I'll cover up your wrong doing if you cover up mine". Defending negative peers. Also includes misplaced loyalty, putting negative peers over positive family or negative family over positive peers. Whether the loyalty issues involve a responsible loyalty deficit (not enough loyalty to the right people or what you know is right) or irresponsible loyalty excess (too much loyalty to the wrong people what you know is wrong), the results are still harmful to self or others.

Helpful opposite- Practice Responsible Loyalty. Be loyal to those who have earned it through their track record of honesty, trustworthiness, concern and responsibility. In relationships, "Think it though" using the reality scales (see p. 24) to help you stand up for what you know is right and who you know is right by: 1) not going along with what is wrong just to get along; 2) not compromising yourself and what you know is right to be accepted by others; 3) not covering up for others wrongdoing (the longer they keep doing wrong, the worse their consequences will be); 4) not picking looks over loyalty in relationships and; 5) not picking negative people over positive ones as friends, "Consider loyalty and faithfulness to be fundamental." (Confucius, c. 551-c. 479 BC).

4. Don't Care Attitude- Examples include… Not caring and not sharing. Includes lack of concern for self by not thinking about consequences before taking action or telling yourself, "I'm only hurting myself". Selfishness- Not thinking about anyone else but yourself. Telling yourself, "Nobody else matters" or "It's every man for himself". Extreme role reversal deficit. Not putting yourself in others shoes or considering the impact of behavior on others. Lacking empathy. Putting others down to build self up. Not sharing with others. Not being socially responsible by being your brother's keeper and sharing your level of awareness i.e., "I shouldn't have to point out problems that others need to change. If I hold myself accountable, that should be enough" A "don't care attitude" about others by those who only care about themselves is only one side of

the coin. Concern problems can also involve excesses with some who have more concern for others than themselves, compromising themselves for others, centering their life around others and thus not really caring enough for self (i.e., "don't care attitude" about self). Whether the concern issues involve a deficit or excess, the results are still harmful to self or others.

Helpful opposite- Show the courage to care, share and try- Take care of yourself and others. Realize that "No act of kindness, no matter how small, is ever wasted" (Aesop, ancient Greek moralist). Let yourself care about what you and do and what is healthy. Help yourself by keeping problems "up front" as a daily priority so that they don't get out of control again. Help others by treating them the way they want to be treated. Push past fears of loss and rejection to let yourself care about others and share your feelings with others who have earned your trust by sharing honest feelings with you. Stop using "who cares" as a face saving excuse not to put effort or energy into getting what you really want. Tell yourself "nothing to it but to do it", push past the fear of failure and try. Add concern to your decision making. Ask yourself, "How will this help/hurt myself or others?" Admit that "If you're not working on the solution, you're part of the problem" and block helplessness by taking responsibility instead of blaming others (i.e., "when you blame other people for your behavior, you give them control over your life"). Use the SET steps to "Solve the Problem" (see p. 25) as opposed to a "don't care attitude" to avoid dealing with the problem.

5. Responsibility Issues- Examples include… <u>No achievement motivation</u>. "I don't need to", "It's not my responsibility", "It's their problem/issue", "I don't want to", puts off doing responsibilities, "I won't because it's not that important", does what they want not what they should. Says they forgot when they ignored it. <u>Not doing their part</u>. Failure to pull own weight. Not <u>"Earning the right to complain"</u> by inconveniencing yourself and finishing a task that was assigned by mistake. <u>Poor work ethic</u>, lazy, "dead beat", borrows and doesn't pay. Feels entitled to top rank pay without starting at the bottom. Includes entitlement dependency attitude, "I don't need to go to school/work" implying that "The world owes me a living". Lack of responsibility motivation involves <u>lack of effort, not finishing what started</u> or finishing but doing half way job. <u>No concept of track record</u> (i.e., telling yourself that you have changed after a few days or weeks when a track record is measured in months and years) is a recovery problem that prevents long term lifestyle change. Puts fun before work is an example of responsibility problem priorities. Also failure to schedule time for responsibilities, and no life achievement goals or motivation to succeed at anything that involves hard work and avoiding responsibilities that are boring or not interesting. Includes "my way" excuses for responsibility refusal, e.g., "I don't have to make it the hard way, I can always… deal drugs, pimp/live off of women, hook/live off of men, go on welfare, depend on my family/friends, gamble or win the lottery". Lack of social responsibility and work effort can be found in the criminal subcultures of societies around the world where realizing that criminal subculture does not represent minority culture determines the unity of these societies. Refusing to accept personal responsibility involving unwillingness to look at ones part in a problem typically involves <u>blaming problems on others or circumstances</u>. Responsibility issues which involve basic responsibility deficits is only one side of the coin with responsibility problems which can also involve excesses by some who take on too much responsibility, do too much for others and blame themselves unnecessarily. Whether the responsibility issues involve a deficit or excess, the results are still harmful to self or others.

Helpful opposite- Accept your responsibilities. "None of us can hope to get anywhere without character, moral courage and the spiritual strength to accept responsibility" (Thomas Watson,

1874-1956). Getting what we want in life requires learning Healthy Behavior Success Skills to **A**void trouble; **C**alm down; **T**hink it through and; **S**olve the problem (see p. 19). These skills help us uphold our responsibilities to maintain self-control, make things right after mistakes (emotional restitution), pull our own weight and learn to accept feedback. Accepting responsibility involves understanding that real men and women have learned to do what they should, when they should for the reason they should. Don't wait for someone to do it for you, try doing it yourself. Take initiative, look for things that need to get done and do them, start your responsibilities without being told and accept reminders. Realize that the only responsible answer when being reminded is, "thank you, I'll take care of that". If you want a break, earn it by finishing what you started or getting to a reasonable quitting point first. Don't get overwhelmed by too much to accomplish. Know that you will get things done if you learn to set and achieve small but realistic goals one at a time. Get honest about being responsible. Admit to yourself that being responsible builds trust which gets you what you want in terms of favors, privileges or promotions. Accept that our number one responsibility is self-control and use "the 3 G's" (i.e., the three-step social responsibility plan, p. 21) to get out of high risk situations and maintain self-control.

6. Blind Ambition- Examples include… Selfishly getting what you want at any cost and not being able to see (being blind to) or consider anything else, including impact on others. "I want what I want when I want it, nothing else matters". In socially irresponsible needs gratification or career achievement, "The ends justify the means" by getting what you want at the expense of others or by putting others at risk for harm. Putting self and career over everything else including family responsibilities, being a selfish "workaholic". Includes flawed definition of achievement and success, using survival as an excuse to exploit others, profit illegally and be a greedy "takeaholic". Putting money over everything. Compromising yourself or your values to get ahead. Being unwilling to accept achievement alternatives that are socially responsible but either require more work or are less rewarding. Blind ambition also includes having "all or nothing thinking" about achievement, ambition or success by adopting an attitude that, "You're either a hero or a zero" or "Second best is the first loser". This thinking focuses you so intensely on ambition that you lose sight of the impact of your behavior (or your absence) on others.

Helpful opposite- Show Socially Responsible Achievement. Examples include looking at possible consequences to self and others not just what you want no matter what. Realize that "You're #1 but there are other numbers" and while it is important to take care of yourself, you have the social responsibility to avoid harming others. Look for win-win solutions where there is benefit for yourself and others. Admit that since doing the right thing takes more effort, you value it more & feel better about it. Ask yourself who really helped you in your life and take on the social responsibility to help someone else. Use the reality scales (p. 24) to weigh what it takes for your success against the severity of what could happen to others. Let go of your all or nothing thinking about ambition, achievement and success. Include "being a better person" by improving your an honesty, trust, loyalty, concern and social responsibility in your personal success goals.

7. Motivational Blindness- Examples include not being aware of why you do what you do. <u>Lacking awareness</u>- Not being aware of feelings that trigger behavior (e.g., anger, anxiety or depression); thoughts that trigger behavior (e.g., using words like "should" or "must" which trigger reactions) or needs that trigger behavior (e.g., for power, acceptance, attention or excitement). Unable to identify and label types of feelings or types of irresponsible thinking. Found yourself saying "I don't know" when asked why you did what you did. Motivational blindness is often reflected by statements like, "It just happened". <u>Lacking understanding</u> about how you got the problem, what maintained it and how it spread to other problems or parts of your life. <u>Closed minded</u>, only paid attention to what you wanted to hear or people who wouldn't bring up your problems. You never really knew you had problems with awareness, understanding and openness. You have heard others say you were "clueless" or therapists say "They don't even know that they don't even know" about you.

Helpful opposite- Develop your Awareness and Insight. Adopt the "Mirror Concept" (p. 125) that "Other people may see you better than you see yourself" and use other people's feedback as a mirror to see yourself. Slow down your reactions and let yourself feel. Then label those feelings. Look at what triggered them to determine where you are coming from with the action you are considering to decide if you really want to take that action. Learn about the Risk Factor Chain that led up to your unhealthy, harmful behavior, the Stress-Relapse Cycle that maintained it and the Harmful Behavior Anatomy that generalized it to other forms and life areas.

8. "I can't" belief (Opposite of Grandiosity)- Examples include… Two basic types- A. <u>Defeatist attitude</u> involving low self-efficacy (confidence) and insecurity. Doesn't believe in abilities. Has unrealistic negative self-appraisal, may be competent but lacks confidence. Doesn't think they are as capable as they actually are, "I can't do it" or "I won't succeed" belief. Feels inferior to others, helpless. Has fear of failure. Afraid to try new things or extend self socially to new people. Extreme pessimism. Always expecting the worst of self and others. Obsessing on the negative. When evaluating the feedback of others, discounting positive feedback and focusing on the negative feedback. "I can't" and "I quit" attitude. Making things fit the "I can't belief by devaluing accomplishments or discounting achievements. B. <u>Resistance to change</u> involving "Hole punching", telling why solutions won't work without trying them or saying they already did when they heard about it but never really gave it a serious try. Says "I can't" when really means "I won't". Gives excuses for not trying.

Helpful opposite- Build your self-confidence. Get honest about the fact that "I can't" may be true but it is really true if you don't get up the courage to try. Start by looking at why you won't try. For example, some people are afraid to try because they are afraid they will fail so they tell themselves "I can't do it so why even try". Others are afraid to put in 100% because if they do their best and don't make it, they are worried about being thought of as a loser or failure. These are excuses to avoid putting in effort to succeed. Get honest with yourself, lose the excuses and put in the effort. Tell yourself the truth. If you try your hardest and don't make it this just means, you didn't succeed at one thing, not that your whole life is a failure. Stop magnifying (p. 125) and start working on the problems in your life. Realize that "If you are not working on the solution, you are part of the problem" and start using your SET problem solving tools (p. 25) to reach your goals.

9. Grandiosity (Opposite of "I can't" Belief)- Examples include… <u>Extreme optimism</u> and unrealistic positive appraisal of self and abilities Discounting constructive feedback from others. Other people notice my abilities and mess with me because they are jealous "haters". Thinks they are more capable than they are. Feels superior to others, arrogant. Overconfidence in abilities, "I can pull this off", "I won't get caught" or "no one will know". "I don't have to avoid high risk situations, I can handle them". "I don't have to plan ahead to avoid problems because I can talk my way out of anything that happens". Highly unrealistic expectations, impatient and intolerant of "stupidity" and sense of entitlement based on view of self as unique and special, e.g., "If I want it, they will want to give it to me" or "Because I like her, she must like me". Extreme entitlement to special attention, privileges, rule exceptions, as a result of uniqueness (e.g., "This doesn't apply to me") or superiority (e.g., "rules are for fools who need others to tell them what to do"). Highly confident but may lack competence.

Helpful opposite- Be Realistic- about what you want, what you need and what people should do for you. Realize that while everyone wants some recognition, no one needs it to survive and no one is likely to recognize your abilities if you don't demonstrate a consistent track record and bring it to their attention. Telling yourself, "They should" recognize my abilities, what I've done, etc, is assuming that others do not have their own world of worries to address. Grandma had a saying about making others aware of your accomplishments, "You've got to toot your own horn because nobody else will". In life, "First do it, then point to it". Be realistic about what you can and can't do. When it comes to doing things you know you shouldn't, get honest about the fact that "no one will know" is usually not true but "Three can keep a secret if two of them are dead" (Benjamin Franklin) is usually true and don't do it. Use the reality scales (see p. 24) to keep grandiosity in check and keep you in touch with the reality of the possible consequences of your actions to yourself and others. Don't over-estimate your self-control ability. Get honest about the fact that staying in high risk situations is likely to trigger relapse and escape trouble with "the 3 G's" (i.e., your three-step responsibility plan, p. 21). Continue to tell yourself that you can do anything that you put your mind to but accept that just thinking about it will not make it happen.

10. Control Issues-

Examples include… "I must be in control" attitude, starting power struggles for fun and to gain control. Plays people against people, rules against rules and concepts against concepts (e.g., being honest vs. being polite to people) to try and get own way. Has attitude of entitlement to do what they want, when they want for the reason they want. Follows Irresponsible Behavior Law, i.e., "What's right is what I want to do and the reason it's right is because I want to do it". Has "Baby My Way" (BMW) fits when they don't get what they want, when they want for the reason they want and reckless BMW driving crashes their relationships. Uses Winning by Intimidation, outbursts to stop others from confronting your behavior, manipulation or any means necessary to get control, continue to do what you want and have things "my way". Self-control motivation deficit and dysfunctional social values, e.g., "It's only wrong if you get caught", "My behavior doesn't bother me so why should I control it?" Physical & verbal bullying, "It's better to be an offender than a victim". "I give ulcers, I don't get them", "I create fear, I don't feel it". "I control other people, they don't control me". Has attitude that power has to do with being in command of (controlling) others not understanding and being in command of (controlling) self & enjoys dominating or manipulating others. Control issues also involve need to control mood or self-medicate by drinking, drugging, eating, spending, sexual indulging or any method that temporarily controls/alleviates unwanted feelings.

Helpful opposite- Work on controlling yourself, not others. Some people who have feelings of helplessness because their lives have been out of control in the past decide to make up for it by controlling others. Others who have been over-controlled (or abused) in the past fall into the "vampire syndrome" and become an over-controlling (or abusive) themselves. Making yourself feel more powerful by over-controlling others results in power struggles or mistreating others and avoids dealing with self. Realize that people who focus too much on being in control could be afraid of feeling helpless often from bad past experiences or repeating what was done to them (the "vampire syndrome"). If any of this applies to you, then conflicts could make you very nervous and too caught up in the extremes of either trying to be in control or trying to avoid conflict. In disagreements or conflicts use the ABC's of letting feelings go to calm down (see page 22) and keep from falling into the extremes of "my way or the highway" or "go along to get along (compromising yourself to be accepted). If past bad memories are triggered by conflicts, remind yourself, "That was then and this is now" and use the reality scales (p. 24) to help you think it through and do the right thing in conflict situations. Decide who you want to run your life, yourself (through decisions you make) or others (who push your emotional buttons and watch you react to feelings they trigger). Get out of those trigger situations, "You need to be laughing and leaving, not staying and stewing". Developing self-control involves using your 3-step social responsibility plan (p. 21) and continually challenging your BMW ("baby my way") thinking, "Why must I always get my way (or always have the last word)?" Weigh out what you are going to say on the reality scales (p. 24) to help you realize that getting "my way" or having the last word is not needed for survival or success and letting it go isn't that severe. Use fantasy fast forward (p. 113) to think ahead by playing the tape in your mind through to the end. Ask yourself, "Is this so important that ten years from now, I will remember not getting my way here?" If the answer is no, let it go. Stop using anger to try and win by intimidation, grow up and admit that anger is a secondary emotion, underneath it you are afraid of not being in control.

11. Image Problems- Examples include… Three basic types- A. <u>Unhealthy pride</u>- Values looking good by being right. Involves unhealthy perfectionism, inability to admit fault, secret keeping and covering up. This is often based on fear of looking bad, stupid, not being accepted or blowing image, by disclosing problems. Reluctant to ask for help, "Keeping up appearances is job #1". B. <u>Criminal pride</u>- Values looking tough/cool. Involves glorifying authority problem tough guy image, viewing kindness as weakness, rules for fools, war story bragging about negative, abusive or criminal behavior and getting over on others, "Being tough is job #1". Criminal pride often involves a fear of being put down and compromising self to fit in, "Being accepted is job #1". C. <u>Superficial values</u>- Valuing what's on the outside (appearance, clothes, jewelry, money) over what's on the inside (honesty, trust, loyalty, concern & responsibility) or who you know over what you know, how you look over how you act. "Looking beautiful/wealthy is job #1". Picking friends based on how that will improve your image or popularity not who is a good person. The superficial values problem of picking looks over loyalty in relationships continues to result in relationship disappointment. All three can involve putting image over integrity, i.e., "Looking good is more important than doing good" and stubborn refusal to back down or change mind.

> **Helpful opposite- Be yourself.** Examples include not trying to be anyone or anything you're not, just being real about your true thoughts and feelings. Your likes are your likes, your opinion is your opinion and your feelings are your feelings. Unless they are unhealthy or harmful, keep them. Attack unhealthy and criminal pride by being yourself and blowing your image with honesty and humor. Use healthy pride by admitting to self that the reason we value honesty so much is the tremendous cost attached to it. Remind yourself that while "Honesty has its price, the good news is you don't have to pay twice". Realize that being yourself uses less energy which decreases stress build up and improves your life. Don't let unhealthy or criminal pride control your behavior, if you were wrong be strong, back down and apologize.

12. Need Problems- Examples include… Three basic types- A. <u>Exaggerated need for acceptance</u>, "I must be accepted" can result in doing too much for others, going along with things that are wrong to be accepted or not be left out (i.e., "going along to get along" and compromising self to be accepted), worrying about how you will be viewed if you do the right thing, tell the truth or if you try something and fail. B. <u>Exaggerated need for excitement</u>, "I need excitement/must be entertained" or "I can't stand boredom" can result in doing risky, unhealthy or harmful behaviors to break boredom or for excitement/fun, putting what is fun before responsibilities, doing something wrong because it is exciting, instigating to spark a conflict or creating chaos with "Drama Queen" exaggerating and emotional amplification. Sparking conflict excitement- the argument is more important than the issue. C. Exaggerated need for attention, "I must get attention" can result in doing something risky, unhealthy or harmful for attention. "Any attention is better than none" and drawing attention to self overshadows the needs of others to also receive social recognition. Can involve getting for Attention for Support or Sympathy.

Helpful opposite- Get a grip on your needs. Realize that attention, acceptance and excitement are human needs not necessities. Everyone wants some degree of attention, acceptance and excitement in their life but no one needs it to survive, no one is entitled to it as a birth right, no one should entertain you, automatically accept you or devote attention to you without getting to know you first. Don't compromise yourself to be accepted, act out for attention or endanger yourself for excitement. If you want acceptance, accept someone. If you want attention, do something good that deserves it. If you want excitement, try something positive that is new and you have never tried before.

13. Planning Problems- Examples include… Not planning ahead or thinking ahead. Putting things off until the last minute, "Not to make a decision is to make a decision". Like motivational blindness, planning problems can be reflected by statements like, "It just happened". Being disorganized, not writing things down and forgetting to turn work in, being late or missing appointments. Not thinking ahead about the possible consequences of taking an action or failing to do a responsibility. Planning problems also involve a planning skills deficit (i.e., never learning how to put priorities in order with the most important responsibilities first), problem priorities (i.e., putting fun or interesting tasks before more important responsibilities) and pathological priorities (putting harmful but exciting activities first such as drinking, drugging or gambling over more important responsibilities such as homework or child care).

Helpful opposite- Use Positive planning, "Think ahead, plan ahead, get ahead." Examples include playing the mental checkers tape, "If I make this move, they will make that move", "If I do this, the result could be that". Use the reality scales (p. 13) to weigh out the consequences of not planning ahead to get things done. Getting yourself together, means getting organized. Each evening after dinner, whether you have been in school, at work or at home, ask yourself, "What do I need to get ready for tomorrow" and get ready by making a list. Good planners are good performers. Humans perform most poorly when they are caught off guard and good planners are rarely caught off guard. Put another way, "If you fail to plan, you plan to fail". With respect to learning social responsibility, accept that "Accidents happen, behaviors are planned and consequences are earned". Use your three SET steps (p. 25- 27) to make success plans for important life goals.

14. Boundary Problems- Examples include… Five basic types: A. Relationship boundary problems- Not enough boundaries, too accepting, highly trustworthy so overly trusting (assumes others are also), getting too involved too quick, violating personal space, touchy feely. Boundaries too defended, problems trusting and/or untrustworthy, too distant, quick to push away, reject or both (i.e., approach-avoidance in relationships, gets too close, too fast, scares self then pulls too far away too fast). Ownership jealousy- viewing a person as property that you own. Objectifying- viewing others as objects to use to get what you want (e.g., sexual abuse). B. Personal boundary problems- Not respecting personal privacy. Nosey, snooping through others possessions, letters, diary wallet, purse, etc. Trying to be in on everything, eavesdropping or

dipping into private conversations, asks inappropriate personal questions. Discloses inappropriate personal information, "Group Leaking", violates group/family therapy confidentiality boundaries (trust abuse). C. Social boundary problems- Viewing elders or superiors as peers and potential partners. Doesn't dress appropriately for age or setting. Acts as if they are a member of a different culture or group. D. Property boundary problems- Property ownership attitude. Theft, borrowing without permission, not returning borrowed property, "What's mine is mine and what's yours is mine" (property abuse), "Give me that!" E. Emotional boundary problems- Doesn't respect other people's feelings by going too far with arguing, teasing horseplay or personal comments. Whether the boundary and trust issues involve a deficit or excess, the results are still harmful to self or others.

Helpful opposite- Show Respect. Treat people like they deserve to be treated. Respect others personal space, personal property, privacy, opinions and feelings. If you want good relationships, take time to get to know the person before getting too involved. If you want to know something personal about someone, ask "Can I ask you a question?" to get them ready. "When in Rome do as the Romans do". This means to respect social boundaries by speaking and acting according to what is appropriate to the setting. For example, if you are at a party and are not Catholic, don't tell jokes about Nuns or Priests. If you want to borrow something from someone and they are not there, don't come back later. Use the reality scales (p. 24) to weigh out how important it is for you to borrow the item in question. If it rates high on the survival or success scales and low on the severity scale (impact on the person you are borrowing from) don't just take it, leave a note and call them as soon as you can. Become aware of your Historical Risk factors in the Risk Factor Chain that led to unhealthy, harmful behavior. Don't transfer your past boundary problems onto present relationships, if you were mistreated, disrespected, devalued or abused put extra effort into respecting others boundaries making sure that others are not treated like servants, property or objects for your personal use.

15. Victim View- Examples include... A preoccupation with injustices, falling into feeling sorry for self and making self miserable in "pity party" ruminating on past issues. Dwelling on past thoughts that reinforce feeling like the victim of things that were not fair. For example, thinking about getting comfort from your mother for the overly harsh discipline of an out of control father that she was too ineffective, depressed or addicted to protect you from or leave. In this regard, the victim view involves rumination (dwelling) on the only two things that can't be changed in life, i.e., the past and other people's behavior. This results in helplessness and a tendency to view self as a victim. The victim view includes attempts to elicit sympathy from others and includes problems accepting personal responsibility, blaming others for your situation, consequences and associated behavior, e.g. "I don't deserve this, it wasn't my fault, they got it started". The victim view can involve the attitude that what happened is either never your fault because someone else got you upset or always your fault because you always mess up. The victim view can also involve being the martyr, trying to get attention for sadness and sympathy. "No one understands" or "You don't understand" or are common victim view responses to those who do understand but just don't agree. Feeling rejected and acting that victim view out was expressed by one young man who said, "It's better to be wanted by the police than not wanted by anyone."

Helpful opposite- Hold yourself Accountable. Let go of your preoccupation with injustices and save your anger for the real injustices. Use the reality scales (p. 24) to help you stop dwelling on the past and other people's behavior. The only two things you can't change in life are the past and other people's behavior. Dwelling on these things makes you feel helpless because you can't change them and feeling helpless keeps your victim view going. Take responsibility for mistakes. Substitute the responsibility tape, (e.g., "What can I do to avoid this in the future?") for the victim rumination tape, (e.g., "This crap ain't right"). Regain control of your life by taking responsibility for your actions. Remind yourself that "It's up to me" to make it in life and "If you blame others for your behavior, you give them control over your life." Stay focused on what you can change (i.e., the present and your behavior), not what you can't change (i.e., the past and other people's behavior). Let go of victim view thinking that, "You don't understand me" and realize that since humans have the same ability to experience feelings it is more likely that they do understand you but simply disagree with your choice in attitude, feelings or behaviors used in your situation. Admit that in the real world, outside of a dysfunctional family, you get consequences as a result of your poor decisions and problem behavior, not because the authorities are taking their bad mood out on you. Put the responsibility for your decisions and behaviors on yourself. Admit that many times you can avoid a problem by avoiding a problem person or a problem place. Accept that , "the best revenge is success" and use your anger from feeling victimized as fuel to succeed by channeling it into getting ahead and making your goals. "If you believe that feeling bad or worrying long enough will change a past or future event, then you are residing on another planet with a different reality system"-- William James (1842- 1910)

16. Justifying Actions

16. Justifying Actions- Includes any form of <u>justifying actions based on feelings</u>. For example, excuses and feelings to justify taking action and avoid taking responsibility for self-control such as "I had to hit him, he really ticked me off!" Justifying harmful actions based on unwanted feelings include hurting others based on anger, hurting self based on depression and avoiding or running from problems based on anxiety. Using feelings to justify taking action and excuse the social responsibility of maintaining self-control of behavior that is harmful to others can be summed up in the statement "They deserved it". On the other hand, justifying unhealthy behavior that is harmful to self (e.g., eating, drinking, smoking, drugs, etc) after successfully handling a stressful situation can be triggered by the self-statement, "I deserve it". Justifying actions based on rationalization includes score keeping and getting even. This irresponsible thinking is often based on incorrect assumption that feelings reflect the way things really are (reality). This can also occur in justifying actions based on beliefs (or group membership), e.g., global, political, religious or gang murder/war. <u>Payback Thinking</u>, i.e., "They wronged me so I'm entitled to my revenge". This type of justification can extend into using relationships for payback, e.g., "You care about them, so I'll hurt you by hurting them" or "You care about me, so I'll hurt you by hurting me". Justifying actions also includes entitlement justification, i.e., "Since they accused me wrongly, I'm entitled to do what they accused me of doing".

Helpful opposite- Follow facts not feelings. Remind yourself that although all feelings are valid experiences, they may not reflect facts and find out the facts before taking action. If action has already been taken, don't justify actions with excuses. Find out the facts and get honest with yourself about what you could have done differently. Realize that payback is a socially irresponsible form of working through anger, hurt or loss. Ask yourself, "In the long run, who really suffers if I do something harmful to myself or get caught for doing something harmful to others?" and "Why should I hurt me just because other people or things hurt me?" Use the ABC's of letting feelings go (p. 12) to calm down, then admit that "The best revenge is success" and move on.

17. Extremism

17. Extremism (Going to Extremes)- Examples include dichotomous (All-or-nothing) thinking. In achievement (school/work/sports) if your performance isn't perfect you're a failure. This is reflected in statements like, "You're either a hero or a zero", "You're a champ or a chump" or "Second best is the first loser". "Being the best is all that counts so if I can't be the best of the best (e.g., student or athlete), I'll be best of the worst (e.g., druggie or bully)". In relationships, "If they don't accept me, I'm a total reject" or being passive, holding things in until stress builds up and blows up through aggressive words or actions. In negotiation, "My way or the highway" view that you must either win or lose and in discussion, "Either you're with me or you're against me". Extremism can include over involvement (encapsulation) in work or relationships to the extreme where everything else is almost excluded or total lack of involvement and detachment, i.e., "It's all in or it's all over". In personal responsibility, extremism can result in viewing problems as either all their fault (which can trigger anger and blaming others unjustly) or all your fault (which can lead to guilt and blaming self unjustly). In parenting discipline, extremism in can result in being too lenient or too harsh which may relate to shifting back and forth between "Don't care attitude" (p. 116) and "Justifying actions based on feelings" (p. 124). Parenting supervision extremism can result in no supervision at all or no freedom at all.

Helpful opposite- Take a Balanced View. Keep your balance in your life goals, relationships, negotiations and opinions. Be very aware of "all or nothing thinking" and how "Don't care attitude" (p. 116) and "Justifying actions based on feelings" (p. 124) triggers going to extremes. Remind yourself that you don't have to be a hero to get recognition from others, that it is unrealistic to expect everyone to agree with you and don't mistake disagreement on an opinion as rejection of you as a person. Understand that it is impossible to always get your way in life, that everyone deserves to get something out of a relationship and it's important to keep a balance of give and take. Take "all things in moderation", strive for the "happy medium" and look for win-win situations in relationships where there are benefits for all involved.

18. Minimizing (Opposite of Magnifying)- Examples include… Playing down problems (often of self) or consequences (often about not doing the right thing). Minimizing behavior frequency or severity can often be identified by the words "Just" or "Only" (e.g., "I just did it once", "I don't do it that much" or "I only yelled, didn't hit them"). Minimizing problems can occur by excusing actions as something you did when you weren't your usual self, "I was really... upset, angry, drunk, high". Minimizing impact or severity can occur by comparison with more serious problems, "It wasn't as bad as what others have done", for example compared to newspaper articles or TV news on the same topic. Minimizing by normalizing (making it seem normal), examples include, "Lots of people do it" or "Everybody does it so it's no big deal".

Helpful opposite- Call it like it is- Use the "Mirror Concept" to avoid minimizing or blocking out valuable feedback from others. The "Mirror Concept" holds that "other people can see you better than you see yourself" and you need to use their feedback as a mirror to get a better view of yourself to avoid minimizing problems. When a mistake has been called to your attention, don't play it down or blow it off. Look at what you need to do to correct the problem, don't try to correct the person. Use feedback to improve your relapse prevention plan, your promise letter and your self-awareness. Don't block feedback out by pointing out that others have made the same mistake. If they made the same mistake and are calling it to your attention, take it serious. They are not a hypocrite because they have done it themselves, they are an expert witness at seeing it because they have done it themselves. Accept that, "It takes one to know one". Keep the focus on the present and your behavior, not the past and others. Substitute getting defensive with the proper response, "Thank you I'll take care of that" to avoid unnecessary conflict.

19. Magnifying (Opposite of Minimizing)- Examples include… Exaggerating a problem (often of others) or consequences (often about doing the right thing). Blowing things way out of proportion, taking constructive feedback personal. Minor criticism is magnified into "disrespect" that is used to justify retaliation. Overgeneralization to the extreme, often used to justify giving up, acting out or not extending self to others, e.g., "since I broke one rule or made one mistake, I'm failing treatment and might as well quit" (rule violation effect), because one adult mistreated you, all adults will mistreat you. Magnifying "Sorry, I couldn't make it, I had to finish my work" into "I'm not interested in you (or you don't matter)" and then stating "You led me on (or lied to me)" as opposed to "I was looking forward to seeing you (or to a visit) and hope to see you soon". Ruminating on injustices, negative feedback or conflicts to the point where any positive is overshadowed and the negative is magnified into triggering action often by using the word "should" or "must". For example, they "should act the way that I want", they "should not have said that" or "I must drink, drug, smoke, eat, spend, hit, cut or run away to get away from my problems and make myself feel better".

    Helpful opposite- Reel it in- Use the "Window Concept" to avoid magnifying feedback from others to the point where you are upset and at risk for acting feelings out. The "Window Concept" involves looking at everything everyone tells you and deciding what to keep. If it's helpful to yourself or others hold it dear to your heart, if it's not, open the window and shovel it out. One way to see the possible benefit of the feedback is to ask yourself, "What if I actually did what the person is saying?" This can make it easier because, "Go to hell!" will not help you but "Shut up while others are talking" will (i.e., we never learn anything while running our mouths). If there is any doubt about whether to keep and apply the feedback you receive, use group consensus (i.e., "If ten people say you're a horse, you're a horse"). Realize that exaggerating problems and stirring up trouble about the behavior of others sends a signal that: you are trying to take the spotlight off of your mistakes; you are a bored drama addict who needs excitement or; a thin skinned insecure person who is hypersensitive to criticism. Ask yourself if you really want to send any of these signals to others. Remind yourself that fighting over disrespect is an admission that you have nothing more valuable to fight for. Use the Reality Scales (p. 24) to weigh out the real seriousness of injustices, negative feedback or conflicts and don't overreact. Use the Reality Scales to put things in perspective and avoid overreaction by weighing out the real seriousness of injustices, negative feedback or conflicts. When a mistake has been called to your attention, don't blow it out of proportion, realize that honest feedback as a way to learn about yourself and grow.

20. Assuming- Examples include… Jumping to conclusions and making assumptions without facts, proof or other evidence to support the assumption. Also involves not verifying your assumption based on initial information by continuing to gather information. Making judgments about others and decisions about actions to take based on unverified assumptions. Not "looking before you leap". Making negative assumptions that because one thing has gone wrong or one error has been made, all is lost and using that as justification to quit trying or give up.

    Helpful opposite- Verify. Realize that things are not always the way they appear so "when in doubt, check it out." Realize that everybody makes mistakes and don't assume that mistakes were on purpose, i.e., "never mistake incompetence for viciousness". When rumors, opinions or other information presented to you kicks up a desire to take action, don't act. If you are being asked or encouraged to act on unverified information use the proper response, "I need to get back to you about that" and then check it out. If you are made to feel that you must take action right away, be creative and come up with a way to check things out or get other opinions before taking action.

Appendix D.   Summary of Situation Response Analysis

The goal of Situation Response Analysis is to increase your self-efficacy (confidence) by learning to analyze your responses to problem situations and by developing your awareness of the Negative Coping that leads to problem responses. Situation Response Analysis is based on the premise that you need to change your internal coping methods (i.e., irresponsible, immature, maladaptive thinking) in order to change your responses to problem situations and break your stress-relapse cycle through positive coping (i.e., responsible, mature, adaptive thinking).

In summary, irresponsible, immature, maladaptive thinking maintains irresponsible, immature, maladaptive emotional and behavioral reactions which in turn tend to be justified by more irresponsible, immature, maladaptive thinking in a continual self-defeating cycle as follows.

- If you always think what you always thought, you will always feel what you always felt.
- If you always feel what you always felt, you will always do what you've always done.
- If you always do what you've always done, you will always think what you've always thought.

Although we all talk to ourselves, that's how we make decisions and solve problems, much of this is automatic and not noticed unless we pay special attention to it. Thus, at first you will probably not be aware of your self-statements (i.e., thinking) that trigger irresponsible, immature or maladaptive reactions to problem situations. Situation Response Analysis is designed to increase your awareness of your thinking during problem situations beginning with helping you review those situations by recording them on a Situation Response Analysis log at the end of each day when you can analyze what needed to be done differently. Consistently analyzing your thinking, associated feelings and reactions to problem situations will help you develop your ability to do "on the spot" substitution of responsible, mature self-statements during actual problem situations. As you begin to develop positive coping through responsible, mature adaptive thinking, you will notice that you are exhibiting less intense emotional reactions and more responsible, mature reactions to problem situations.

Situation	Response	Analysis	
Date and what actually happened in the situation (the facts). People, places, things, sights, sounds or other experiences that triggered irresponsible thinking, unwanted feelings or unhealthy, harmful behavior urges/cravings.	Your response to the situation. What you said to yourself (thoughts), what you were feeling (emotions) and what you did (behavior- What you said to others and what actions you took).	Your analysis of your response to the situation in two areas: 1) whether it was positive and helpful or; 2) negative and harmful and; 3) what you need to do next time.	
	Thoughts, Feelings, Behavior	**Positive Coping (1)**	**Negative Coping (2)**
		Positive Planning (3) What you need to say to yourself (or do) next time. How you will use Responsible Self-statement Substitution or your ACTS skills next time.	

1. This is what you need to say to yourself or do after the Situation to avoid trouble (responsible, adaptive thinking that prevents unhealthy, harmful behavior. Positive Coping is the socially responsible, mature approach to problem situations that decreases destructive urges, making appropriate social behavior control easier. Using any of your ACTS skills to Avoid trouble, Calm down, Think it through and Solve the problem is positive coping. Remember to use your ACTS skills in order during a crisis situation because you can't "Calm down" and "Think it through" when overwhelmed by a high risk situation trigger. You have to Avoid trouble by getting out first.

2. This is what you said to yourself after the Situation that led to the irresponsible, immature, maladaptive Response that causes problems for yourself and/or others. Negative Coping through maladaptive thinking includes irresponsible thinking, irrational beliefs, inaccurate attributions and perceptions. Irrational beliefs are unrealistic expectations (e.g., irrational use of "should" or "must"). Inaccurate attribution is responsibility, cause or blame that you attributed or assigned to yourself or others by mistake, for example jumping to conclusions by "assuming" things that can't be proved for certain and acting on them without waiting to find the facts. Inaccurate perceptions are views, opinions and feelings about yourself or others that are not correct, for example viewing the situation as less serious than it really us (i.e., using the words "just" or "only").

3. If you used positive coping- Positive planning involves rewarding yourself for doing the right thing and telling someone about your accomplishment (if in a group program writing an accomplishment award on yourself). If you used negative coping- Positive planning involves responsible self-statement substitution by identifying the irresponsible thinking you used (or actions you took) and substituting the responsible thinking you need to use next time. Write what you need to say to yourself (responsible self-statement substitution) or do next time to avoid falling into problems. Hint: For what you need to say to yourself, review "Responsible Self-statement Substitution 101" (p. 67). For what you need to do, think about which one of your healthy relationship or behavior (ACTS) success skills could have helped (p. 11- 16). Write how you could apply any of these success skills next time.

Be sure to make at least one Situation Response Analysis log entry every day as you will be using what you learned from this log in treatment and all three workbooks.

SRT Appropriate Social Behavior Control Exercise

Developing awareness of high risk situations and irresponsible thinking is the first step towards appropriate social behavior control of urges that can result in harmful behavior. Here are some examples in order of seriousness...

Uncontrolled Urge	Resulting Abusive Behavior
Anxious urge to cover-up mistakes or Grandiosity urge to get over on someone	Trust Abuse (lying, deceiving, misleading, omitting)
Negative mood urge, sensation urge (sight, smell) or peer acceptance urge to get high, overeat, smoke	Substance Abuse (drugs, alcohol, tobacco, food)
Envy urge to take or break	Property Abuse (theft, vandalism)
Aggressive urge to get even or get "my way"	Physical Abuse (punch, kick, slap, threaten)
Sexual excitement urge to have sex	Sexual Abuse (rape, child molesting, peer coercion)

Many people in treatment relapse and commit another abusive behavior as a result of entering high risk situations and using irresponsible thinking as opposed to positive coping in those situations. Here are some examples in order of seriousness…

High Risk Situation	Resulting Urge & Irresponsible Thinking
Getting confronted about doing something wrong or making a mistake	Anxious urge to cover-up mistakes or Grandiosity urge to get over on someone, e.g., "I can't stand the consequences so I have to lie"
Being around peers who ask you to get high with them. Smelling weed, cigarettes or food	Negative mood urge or peer acceptance urge to get high, smoke or eat, e.g., "One last time won't hurt"
Hearing someone brag about what they have and feeling inferior or less than them	Envy urge to take or break, e.g., "They can afford t lose it" or "They deserve it for showing off"
Continuing to stick around and listen to someone who is putting you down	Aggressive urge to get even, e.g., "The need to be taught a lesson" or "I'll show you"
Starring at a person that is sexually attractive or at porno, Listening to sex talk or 900 toll calls.	Sexual excitement urge to have sex, e.g., "It's just sex, everybody does it"

Irresponsible Thinking in High Risk Situations: The Candy Bar Exercise

In real estate, the key to good property value is location, location and location. In harmful behavior treatment, the key to relapse is access, access and access (to high risk people, places or things). Since you must learn to identify and eliminate your irresponsible thinking in high risk situations in order to prevent relapse, this exercise is designed to generate some irresponsible thinking for you to address on your Situation Response Analysis log. Bring in your favorite candy bar and have your therapist sign and date it. You will be using your candy bar to represent your high risk situation as a structured exercise to help you discover the thinking that leads a person to relapse when in a high risk situation. Your self-control goal is to turn your candy bar back in next week unopened with no part eaten. You are to carry your candy bar on you at all times in a place where it will not melt. No excuses will be accepted, if you lost it, it will be assumed that you caved into your urge and ate it. Use your Situation, Response, Analysis Log to help you become aware of the high risk situation triggers (thoughts, feelings) that relate to urges along with the positive and negative coping that you use in when in a high risk situation. Discuss your logs with your therapist or group if you are in treatment. This assignment will be evaluated with equal weight applied to how well you complete your logs and how much of your candy bar you turn in next week. Good luck on learning to become aware of the irresponsible thinking related to urges to eat your favorite candy bar! You may need to use a different object (see note).

Note: If you are in treatment for food abuse, are diabetic, are allergic to candy bar ingredients, have had bariatric surgery which could trigger dumping syndrome or have any condition that could harm you by eating your favorite candy bar, do not begin this exercise without making an informed decision after consulting your therapist about the potential benefits & possible adverse impact of participation. If you are advised to use a different object or an empty candy bar, empty it during a treatment session, discuss the thoughts/feelings triggered by throwing food away and use that information as your first SRA log entry.

Social Responsibility Therapy

Situation Response Analysis Log   Name: _____

Situation	Response	Analysis
Date & Description (What actually happened)	**My Thoughts, Feelings and Behavior**	1. Was my response positive/helpful or negative/harmful? 2. What do I need to do in this situation next time?
	Thoughts- Feelings*- Behavior-	**Thoughts:** ___ Positive Coping; ___ Negative Coping **Feelings:** ___ Tolerable; ___ Stressful; ___ Unbearable **Behavior:** ___ Healthy/helpful; ___ Unhealthy/harmful **My positive plan for next time is...**
	Thoughts- Feelings*- Behavior-	**Thoughts:** ___ Positive Coping; ___ Negative Coping **Feelings:** ___ Tolerable; ___ Stressful; ___ Unbearable **Behavior:** ___ Healthy/helpful; ___ Unhealthy/harmful **My positive plan for next time is...**
	Thoughts- Feelings*- Behavior-	**Thoughts:** ___ Positive Coping; ___ Negative Coping **Feelings:** ___ Tolerable; ___ Stressful; ___ Unbearable **Behavior:** ___ Healthy/helpful; ___ Unhealthy/harmful **My positive plan for next time is...**
	Thoughts- Feelings*- Behavior-	**Thoughts:** ___ Positive Coping; ___ Negative Coping **Feelings:** ___ Tolerable; ___ Stressful; ___ Unbearable **Behavior:** ___ Healthy/helpful; ___ Unhealthy/harmful **My positive plan for next time is...**

* Rate any cravings/urges to eat, drink, drug, smoke, gamble, fight, get sex (1-10: 1=mild urge, 5=moderate urge, 10=very strong urge)

Appendix E.   Social Responsibility Therapy Self-Evaluation

Do a self-evaluation of your social-emotional maturity progress in each of the areas below.

Name: _____   **Date:** _____

Honesty (check one and explain): __improved; __problems; __both.

_____

_____

_____

Trust (check one and explain): __improved; __problems; __both.

_____

_____

Loyalty (check one and explain): __improved; __problems; __both.

_____

_____

Concern (check one and explain): __improved; __problems; __both.

_____

_____

Responsibility (check one and explain): __improved; __problems; __both.

_____

_____

_____

Self-Awareness (check one and explain): __improved; __problems; __both.

_____

_____

Self-Efficacy/Confidence (check one and explain): __improved; __problems; __both.

_____

_____

Self-Control (check one and explain): __improved; __problems; __both.

_____

_____

_____

Appendix F.
Awareness and Honesty Examination

"We cannot solve our problems with the same thinking we used when we created them."--Albert Einstein

Name: _____   **Date**: _____

Cognitive Risk Factors involve Irresponsible Thinking that supports and allows irresponsible behavior that is harmful to self or others. Responsible Thinking supports responsible behavior that is helpful to self or others. Irresponsible behavior is associated with being immature and means not acting responsible by doing the right thing at the right time for the right reason. Irresponsible people do what they want, when they want for the reason they want without thinking about whether their actions could be harmful to self or others. Irresponsible thinking that supports and allows unhealthy, harmful behavior includes thinking errors, irrational beliefs, false conclusions, false perceptions and cognitive disinhibitors (thoughts that disinhibit or break down your resistance to unhealthy, harmful behavior). In order to substitute more appropriate, responsible thinking, you need to become aware of the irresponsible thinking that supports and allows harmful behavior. Irresponsible thinking increases the risk of harmful behavior by justifying or minimizing dwelling on harmful behavior thoughts or plans, entering or staying in high risk situations for harmful behavior, or pushing back the line on what you know is wrong and heading for trouble. Not being aware of Irresponsible Thinking puts you at risk for repeating behavior that is harmful to yourself or others.

Awareness and Honesty Examination

Self-awareness and honesty about yourself is very important in your treatment. The following "Awareness and Honesty Examination" is made up of questions designed to see *how aware you are* of the way you think, act and talk to yourself along with *how honest you can be* about your thoughts, feelings and behavior. Everyone makes mistakes and has problems dealing with things that happen to them from time to time. Everyone slips and does things they shouldn't even though they have a feeling that what they are considering may be wrong.

The following Awareness and Honesty Examination covers cognitive risk factors along with social responsibility problems that support harmful behavior and prevent getting the most out of treatment. The items on this exam include ways that people think and act when handling unfortunate events, making mistakes, getting in trouble, conflicts or doing something they shouldn't that could be harmful to self or others.

Taking this exam is the exact opposite of the typical classroom test, job interview or first date where the object is to make yourself look good in order to "score" highly or do well in making a positive impression. In this task, since the object is self-awareness and honesty, "When you're looking bad, you're looking good", that is when you are aware of shortcomings or problem areas and get honest about them (i.e., look bad), you get the highest honesty and awareness score (i.e., look good). Think about each question and mark it if you are aware of it or if you have been made aware of it by others (told that you do it or confronted about it).

When dealing with past situations, please rate how often you have had the following thoughts or behaviors.

Use the numbered ratings on the scale below to rate your answers to the following questions.

0	1	2	3	4
Never	Sometimes	Half of the time	Often	Almost Always

When dealing with past situations, please rate how often you have...

___ 1. Told others what you thought they wanted to hear, not exactly what happened.

___ 2. Not being polite to others while expecting or demanding respect for yourself.

___ 3. Held on to a relationship where you put in more than you got out.

___ 4. Told yourself or others that "you've got to look out for number one" because nobody else will or thought that in life it's "every man for himself".

___ 5. Told yourself "I give up, there's no use in trying".

___ 6. Said "I forgot" or "you forgot to tell me" when reminded about something you knew you were supposed to do.

___ 7. Told yourself that becoming successful is more important than anything else in life.

___ 8. Not been exactly sure why you have done some of the things that you did.

___ 9. Told yourself that you will stay in control and never let anyone hurt you, take advantage of you or get the best of you again.

___ 10. Felt I could do anything if I wasn't held back by others or situations.

___ 11. Felt that people would look down on you if you showed your emotions, admitted you were wrong or admitted a mistake.

___ 12. Went along with things you wouldn't normally do or that you knew were wrong in order to fit in, be accepted, be socially comfortable or avoid being put down.

___ 13. Not written down things that needed to get done and didn't get them turned in or completed.

___ 14. Borrowed things without asking or forgot to return borrowed items.

___ 15. Told yourself that what you did wasn't that bad because you did it on rare occasions, when stressed out or when using drugs/alcohol.

___ 16. Told yourself or others that what happened wasn't your fault because someone else got you upset or you always get blamed whether you did wrong or not.

___ 17. Justified actions based on feelings- For example, told yourself the other person deserved what you said or did because they got you upset or told yourself that you deserved to do something harmful (eating, drinking, smoking, drugs) because you were upset.

___ 18. Thought that if people aren't with you, they're against you.

___ 19. Jumped to conclusions based on how the situation looked at the time.

___ 20. Told yourself or others that a problem others caused or mistake they made was worse than it really was and made a big deal about it.

0 Never	1 Sometimes	2 Half of the time	3 Often	4 Almost Always

When dealing with past situations, please rate how often you have...

___ 21. Said "Yes" to someone with no intention of doing what they ask.

___ 22. Multiplied criticism you received by two (telling yourself it was really harsh) while dividing the criticism you gave in half (telling yourself you weren't that harsh).

___ 23. Put negative peers/friends before family or positive, responsible peers.

___ 24. Been told or thought that you don't care how your actions might affect others.

___ 25. Felt that things always go wrong and will never work out.

___ 26. Not tried your hardest and done things half way or just enough to get by.

___ 27. Put getting ahead, work or making money (including illegally) before family or friends.

___ 28. Not been aware of feeling any certain way (e.g., sad, anxious, angry) when upset over something.

___ 29. Felt very upset when things didn't go the way you wanted them to and told yourself "This is terrible" or "I can't stand this".

___ 30. Been annoyed by people who know less than me trying to tell me what to do.

___ 31. Found yourself worrying about being put down, looking bad, being embarrassed or messing up in front of others.

___ 32. Done something risky or wrong for attention.

___ 33. Been told that you are not organized.

___ 34. Let joking, teasing or horseplay go too far.

___ 35. When considering doing something wrong or explaining what you did to others, found yourself using the words, "just", "only", "a little", "rarely" or "once".

___ 36. Felt that you couldn't help yourself from getting in trouble because you were encouraged or the other person started it.

___ 37. Given others logical explanations that excuse or justify a mistake you made.

___ 38. Felt like "You're either a hero or a zero", that there is nothing in between and anything less than being number one is not good enough.

___ 39. Made decisions without consulting others because the motivations, attitudes or actions of those involved were clear and there was no need to check out the information that was presented.

___ 40. Told yourself or others that a mistake that you made was horrible, made a big deal out of it and turned it into a really upsetting experience.

___ 41. Left out parts of a story or told the part of a mistake, error or problem that wasn't so bad and left out parts that were worse.

___ 42. Told yourself that trust should be given to you without considering that your trust in others is earned by their behavior.

0	1	2	3	4
Never	Sometimes	Half of the time	Often	Almost Always

When dealing with past situations, please rate how often you have...

___ 43. Defended negative, irresponsible peers or partners that really didn't deserve my support.

___ 44. Told yourself that your behavior only hurts you or if you knew it affected others told yourself "it could be worse".

___ 45. Felt a lack of confidence in yourself.

___ 46. Been told that you are unmotivated or lazy about doing anything you don't want to do (including paying back money you borrow).

___ 47. Told yourself or others that you will do anything it takes to get ahead.

___ 48. Found yourself saying "I don't know" to people who asked you why you did what you did and not really caring to think about it.

___ 49. Played people against people to try and get what you wanted.

___ 50. Felt people have been jealous of your unique and special qualities or talents.

___ 51. Felt that people judge you on your looks so looking good is the most important thing.

___ 52. Gone along with others & made fun of someone that you get along with & think are OK.

___ 53. Had problems because of not thinking ahead about the possible consequences of taking an action or failing to do a responsibility.

___ 54. Found yourself listening in on interesting conversations, asking personal questions or looking through others stuff that they left out.

___ 55. Said to yourself or others "It wasn't that wrong", "It didn't do that much harm", "Others have done it also" or "It wasn't as bad as what others have done".

___ 56. Felt that the situation wasn't fair, you weren't given a chance or you didn't deserve what Happened ("This isn't right") after not doing well or making a mistake.

___ 57. Made a mental list of why what you did was OK or why it will be OK for you to do something that you really shouldn't.

___ 58. Felt like if it can't be done perfectly, why do it at all (or if it can't be done just right, it's not worth doing).

___ 59. Thought that because one thing went wrong or one mistake was made, everything is blown and you might as well quit trying.

___ 60. Told yourself or others that a consequence you received was worse than what really occurred.

___ 61. Lied, misled others or covered things up in order to avoid possible consequences.

___ 62. Considered mistakes you made as accidents but were more likely to view mistakes others made as on purpose.

___ 63. Covered for someone who has covered for you or kept negative secrets for and with others to cover up problems or mistakes.

___ 64. Been called selfish by a peer, associate, friend, family member or significant other.

0	1	2	3	4
Never	Sometimes	Half of the time	Often	Almost Always

When dealing with past situations, please rate how often you have...

___ 65. Told yourself or others excuses for why you can't do something that you are able to do but just don't want to do.

___ 66. Told yourself that the problem was with the job, class or person instead of your ability to handle frustration or disappointment.

___ 67. Been told that when it comes to getting what you want, you don't worry about anyone getting hurt but yourself.

___ 68. Thought things just seem to happen to you for no reason that you have no control over.

___ 69. Showed anger towards others (i.e., sarcasm, annoyance, intimidation, threats or aggressive behavior), used coercion, bribery or manipulation in order to try to get what you wanted.

___ 70. Have had total confidence in your ability to talk your way out of problems or situations.

___ 71. Felt that since people view kindness as weakness, being tough is necessary to get respect.

___ 72. Done something risky or wrong for excitement.

___ 73. Told yourself "Live for today, not for tomorrow" and made your plans based on your needs right now without considering the future effects of your decisions.

___ 74. Been jealous in a relationship, possessive or not wanted others to socialize with someone you really like.

___ 75. Told yourself "Others did it with me (or got me into it) and I'm still alive so it's not that bad if I get others involved".

___ 76. Told yourself or others "He/she did it" or "They caused this problem" when you also had something to do with it.

___ 77. Worked yourself up (e.g., "This isn't right") and then followed your feelings into getting even (e.g., "I'll show you").

___ 78. Thought that "If I can't be the best of the best, I'll be the best of the worst".

___ 79. Assumed that if what you said or did was really a problem, someone would bring it to your attention.

___ 80. Exaggerated or blown something that happened to you so far out of proportion that it was absurd or silly.

___ 81. Been vague with others in order to avoid possible problems.

___ 82. Not asked for help because you thought you should be able to do it on your own or that asking for help shows that you are weak.

___ 83. Complained about others responsibility problems before completing your own.

___ 84. Counted on people who couldn't be counted on and been let down or disappointed.

___ 85. Said negative things about others or put them down when they were not present to hear what you were saying.

___ 86. Felt like I would never be able to succeed in my life goals.

0	1	2	3	4
Never	Sometimes	Half of the time	Often	Almost Always

When dealing with past situations, please rate how often you have...

___ 87. Told yourself "It can wait", "I can do this later" or other excuses to put off doing responsibilities.

___ 88. Told yourself that you had to take what you want or use emotions such as anger, tears or guilt trips to get what you want if asking doesn't work.

___ 89. Paid attention to what you liked (i.e., agreeable feedback from others) and ignored what you didn't want to hear (i.e., disagreeable feedback).

___ 90. Argued to try and win control of the situation or just for the fun of the struggle.

___ 91. Have been 100% confident that I could control or handle problems without making any mistakes.

___ 92. Told yourself or others that being afraid is a weakness.

___ 93. Didn't plan ahead and put things off until the last minute.

___ 94. Stirred up an argument or started a conflict to break up the boredom.

___ 95. Got involved quickly in a relationship that didn't work out.

___ 96. Told yourself or others "You don't understand me".

___ 97. Been told that you are not doing your part of work or family responsibilities or felt that you are not pulling your own weight.

___ 98. Compared yourself to others on TV or the newspaper and thought that other people have a lot more problems.

___ 99. Told yourself "What I'm doing is OK because I'm not really hurting anyone but myself".

___ 100. Told yourself that most things are not accidents and what goes wrong is either your fault or their fault.

___ 101. Kept silent in order to avoid having to discuss a problem.

___ 102. Not spoken up about a problem because you didn't want to be viewed as a "snitch" or felt it was none of your business.

___ 103. Thought that you should be given a chance and trusted but haven't really trusted others.

___ 104. Had something that was done wrong to you (or someone you care about) go over and over in your mind, not been able to let it go.

___ 105. Told yourself that your behavior isn't really a harmful problem and if it does effect you "look at the bright side, it could be worse".

___ 106. Found yourself avoiding responsibilities that you find boring or disagreeable.

___ 107. Been told that you don't see things from anyone else's point of view but your own.

___ 108. Got others in trouble or did something to get even because they said or did something to you.

___ 109. Felt that others were better than me in one way or another.

0	1	2	3	4
Never	Sometimes	Half of the time	Often	Almost Always

When dealing with past situations, please rate how often you have...

____ 110. Told yourself "the best way to deal with problems is to put them out of my mind" .

____ 111. Been late to or missed important appointments.

____ 112. Realized you got too close too quick in a relationship and pulled back fast to get some space.

____ 113. Found yourself getting angry at others and pointing out their problems/issues after they give you some criticism.

____ 114. Thought that unless there is a good chance of achieving your goal right away, it's not worth trying.

____ 115. Felt that I should get more support, attention and concern from others.

____ 116. Told yourself "Even if my behavior is somewhat harmful, lots of people do it" or "Since I only did with others who have already done it before, it's not that bad".

____ 117. Changed the subject or quickly skipped over to another topic when asked about a problem or mistake.

____ 118. Told yourself or others, "If you care about me you should trust me" or used, "You don't trust me" to get your way.

____ 119. Put someone down because what they did or said was dumb from your point of view.

____ 120. Felt there's no real need to change or listen to those who say they want to help me or lashed out at those trying to help me.

____ 121. Put doing something fun before doing responsibilities or work.

____ 122. Ignored what others said without even giving it consideration because you already knew what you were going to do so why even listen.

____ 123. Told yourself "I couldn't ask because they might have said no".

____ 124. Told yourself or others that you were not afraid when you really were.

____ 125. Told yourself that others should cooperate and go along with you more than they do or been disappointed at others lack of cooperation with you.

____ 126. Considered yourself more mature for your age and looked at older people as equals, friends or possible dating partners (now or at any time in your life).

____ 127. Didn't speak up about a problem or tell others what they should know because I didn't want to get someone in trouble or thought "what they don't know won't hurt them".

____ 128. Found yourself looking for support and affection more than looking for the opportunity to give it to others.

____ 129. Told yourself "Even if my behavior is a problem sometimes, it's a free country so if others don't like it they can hang out with someone else. If they hang around me and something bad happens that effects them, it's their own fault for staying."

____ 130. Complained about aches, pains and a lack of energy to get responsibilities done.

0	1	2	3	4
Never	Sometimes	Half of the time	Often	Almost Always

When dealing with past situations, please rate how often you have...

___ 131. Told yourself that you can't learn from people that you don't like or you shouldn't have to listen to people you don't like.

___ 132. Told yourself or others "Why are they lying?" and assuming that others must be lying because they are not reporting things the way you view them.

___ 133. Brought up the problems of others or put them down to make yourself look better.

___ 134. Told yourself it's better to be an offender than a victim (pick on others as opposed to be picked on, take advantage of others as opposed to be conned).

___ 135. Trusted people that seemed OK but you haven't known for long by telling them personal things about yourself or others and been let down.

___ 136. Brought up something to get people arguing and take the heat off of yourself when being confronted about a problem.

___ 137. Insisted that others let you in on things but kept the information you had to yourself.

___ 138. Told yourself that if you can't get a high paying job, it's better not to work at all.

___ 139. Not bothered to pay any attention at all unless the person got your attention by raising their voice or calling everyone's attention to you.

___ 140. Thought that if people don't agree with me, they are probably trying to put me down in front of others because they don't like me.

___ 141. Been angry at others for not trusting you without asking any questions.

___ 142. Told yourself that if you want to maintain the respect of others, you can't back down even on little points.

___ 143. Shifted to another friend for support after a disagreement to let things "cool off".

___ 144. Admitted to a less serious problem or mistake to get people off of the track when asked about a more serious problem or mistake.

___ 145. Been angry at others for shifting their loyalty to other friends or for cheating when you have done the same.

___ 146. Asked yourself why people bother you about finishing things that they could do themselves if it was really that important.

___ 147. Thought that only someone that has had my kind of problem can understand me and help me.

___ 148. Showing anger about being accused without carefully listening to or thinking about the other persons point of view.

___ 149. Felt that if you admit a mistake to others they will probably use it against you.

___ 150. Pointed out what others who were involved did or that others do it too, in order to take the heat off of yourself.

___ 151. Told yourself that if you are working on a problem area and do something right, people should recognize your accomplishment and treat you like you have changed as opposed to saying "Let's see if you can keep it up".

0	1	2	3	4
Never	Sometimes	Half of the time	Often	Almost Always

When dealing with past situations, please rate how often you have...

____ 152. When someone in authority was talking, found yourself ignoring them.

____ 153. Told yourself or others that people can't be trusted so it is always best to keep things to yourself.

____ 154. Confronted others honesty without first getting honest yourself.

____ 155. Have been told or thought that you have had problems finishing what you started.

____ 156. Felt that if others don't go along or cooperate with you like they should, you will have to do something about it or take things into your own hands and/or told yourself, "It's only wrong if you get caught".

____ 157. Thought that people with the same problems that I have are no better off than me and have no right to act like they can help me.

____ 158. Added unnecessary facts or statements to a story (i.e., purposefully made it too long or got it off track) in order to take the focus off of the main issue and avoid problems.

____ 159. Complained about unfair responsibility assignments before completing them.

____ 160. Told yourself that if others don't keep track of their things, they don't really care about them so there's no need to return those things unless asked.

Please list and other thoughts or things that you say to yourself that have caused past problems. Add feedback from your treatment group, therapist, family or partner about their view.

_____

_____

_____

_____

Look over your ratings. List any patterns or connections that you notice on the items you rated.

_____

_____

_____

Go over your answers to the Awareness and Honesty questions to make sure that you have been completely accurate. Then make a photocopy of these results and turn them into your therapist before continuing any further assignments in this workbook.

I have answered this examination honestly and to the best of my ability without any attempt to make myself look better or worse than my past behavior would indicate.

Signature: _____   **Date Completed**: _____

Social Responsibility Therapy for Adolescents and Young Adults
A Multicultural Treatment Manual for Harmful Behavior
James M. Yokley, Ph.D.

Table of Contents
Chapter 1. Social Responsibility Therapy
Overview, Intervention Evidence Base and
Multicultural Approach. **Chapter 2.** Client Awareness
Training: The Problem Development Triad. **Chapter 3.**
Social Responsibility Therapy Implementation
Methods and Treatment Protocol. **Chapter 4.**
Research Support for Social Responsibility Therapy
Methods & Procedures. Notes. References.

About the Author
James M. Yokley, Ph.D., is a Clinical Psychologist on
the medical staff in the Department of Psychiatry at
MetroHealth Medical Center in Cleveland, Ohio, as well
as an Assistant Professor at Case Western Reserve
University School of Medicine and Department of
Psychology. He has expertise in cognitive-behavior
therapy with multiple forms of unhealthy, harmful
behavior, has authored over 50 research publications,
book chapters, and professional presentations, and
is a regular conference speaker on this topic.

Paperback: 978-0-7890-3121-1. $49.95 • May
2008, 357pp

Social Responsibility Therapy for Adolescents and
Young Adults: A Multicultural Treatment Manual
for Harmful Behavior provides a comprehensive
explanation of Social Responsibility Therapy, its
advantages, and the intervention evidence-base
for multiple forms of harmful behavior. This text
discusses in detail the multicultural intervention
approach, its rationale, and content.
Implementation methods and treatment protocol
are explored. The book includes illustrated case
studies, tables, figures, and references to
additional available readings.

Topics discussed in Social Responsibility Therapy
for Adolescents and Young Adults: A Multicultural
Treatment Manual for Harmful Behavior include:

• evidence-based procedures used in Structured
  Discovery learning experiences to target harmful
  behavior
• helping clients discover how they acquired,
  maintained, and generalized a broad range of
  harmful behavior
• addressing target behavior problems, negative
  social influence problems, and the dose-
  response problem
• five areas of human functioning that are critical
  to the wellbeing of self and others which can
  only be addressed through psychotherapy and
  forensic parenting
• developing prosocial behavior alternatives which
  contribute to both relapse prevention and
  personal development and much more!

Social Responsibility Therapy for Adolescents and
Young Adults: A Multicultural Treatment Manual
for Harmful Behavior is an essential resource for
social workers, counselors, psychologists, and
psychiatrists whose caseloads include a
multicultural population of young people who
exhibit multiple forms of unhealthy, harmful
behavior.

Order online through
www.socialsolutionspress.com

Social Responsibility Therapy for Adolescents and Young Adults
A Multicultural Treatment Manual for Harmful Behavior
James M. Yokley, Ph.D.

"A valuable contribution to the field, confronting important issues at the psychological and societal levels. Provides a comprehensive framework for managing some of the most challenging clinical problems. Provides useful guidelines for promoting prosocial values and behaviors in delinquent youth. The treatment strategies balance the notions of therapeutic structure with client discovery. Many interesting and provocative quotations are laced throughout the text. A valuable addition to any library."
    —James C. Overholser, PhD, ABPP, professor of psychology,
    director of clinical training, Case Western Reserve University

Social Responsibility Therapy for Adolescents and Young Adults: A Multicultural Treatment Manual for Harmful Behavior is a crucial treatment manual for mental health professionals whose caseloads include a multicultural population of adolescents and young adults who exhibit multiple forms of harmful behavior. This unique therapy enhances relapse prevention in harmful behavior treatment by addressing the target behavior problem, negative social influence problem, dose-response problem, and the behavior migration problem. It also acknowledges that harmful behavior is multicultural, and it addresses the key criticisms of multicultural therapy through a theory-driven treatment approach that utilizes methods and procedures from existing evidence-based treatments with known multicultural applications.

This text provides a comprehensive explanation of Social Responsibility Therapy, its advantages, and the intervention evidence-base for multiple forms of harmful behavior. It discusses in detail the multicultural intervention approach, its rationale, and content; describes the implementation methods and treatment protocol; and includes illustrated case studies, tables, figures, and references to additional readings. This book is an essential resource for mental health professionals from all disciplines, including social workers, counselors, psychologists, and psychiatrists who are involved in the treatment of multiple forms of harmful behavior.

James M. Yokley, PhD, is a clinical psychologist in the Department of Psychiatry at MetroHealth Medical Center in Cleveland, Ohio, and is an assistant professor at Case Western University School of Medicine and Department of Psychology.

Routledge
Taylor & Francis Group

www.routledgementalhealth.com

Printed in the U.S.A.
Cover design: Elise Weinger Halprin

ISBN: 978-0-7890-3121-1

an **informa** business

The Social Responsibility Therapy:
Understanding Harmful Behavior Workbook Series

The Social Responsibility Therapy workbook series on Understanding Harmful Behavior was designed to help individuals with unhealthy, harmful behavior understand how they got that problem, what kept it going and how it spread to other areas through "The Problem Development Triad".

Workbook 1- "How did I get this problem?" focuses on understanding how unhealthy, harmful behavior was acquired through "The Risk Factor Chain". ISBN: 978-0-9832449-0-5.

Workbook 2- "Why do I keep doing this?" focuses on understanding how unhealthy, harmful behavior problems were maintained by "The Stress-Relapse Cycle". ISBN: 978-0-9832449-1-2.

Workbook 3- "How did my problem spread?" focuses on understanding how unhealthy, harmful behavior problems were generalized to other areas using "The Harmful Behavior Anatomy". ISBN: 978-0-9832449-2-9.

The Clinician's Guide to Social Responsibility Therapy:
Practical Applications, Theory and Research Support

The Clinician's Guide to Social Responsibility Therapy: Practical Applications, Theory and Research Support (ISBN-978-0-9832449-4-3) supplements the Social Responsibility Therapy Treatment Manual for Adolescents & Young Adults (Yokley, 2008) by providing:
1) Practical clinical applications, case examples and exercises illustrating the treatment model;
2) A positive lifestyle change description integrating theory, research support and practical examples and; 3) Clinician support for using the three Social Responsibility Therapy workbooks described above on understanding and managing unhealthy, harmful behavior.

Further description and order information is available at
www.socialsolutionspress.com

For volume or non-profit organization discounts, e-mail order information (Name, zip code and number of workbooks, organization and population served) to...
info@socialsolutionspress.com

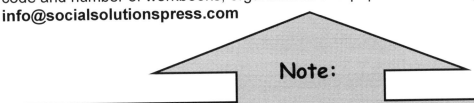

Note:

Social Responsibility Therapy is a
Social Solutions Healthy Behavior Lifestyle Project

www.srtonline.org   www.socialsolutionspress.com   www.forensicare.org

Made in the USA
Middletown, DE
04 September 2017